MULTICULTURALISM IN COUNSELING

MULTICULTURALISM IN COUNSELING

DANIEL T. SCIARRA
Hofstra University

F. E. Peacock Publishers, Inc.
Itasca, Illinois

Copyright © 1999
F. E. Peacock Publishers, Inc.
All rights reserved
Library of Congress Catalog Card No. 98-68252
ISBN 0-87581-420-5
Printed in the U.S.A.
10   9   8   7   6   5   4   3   2   1
04   03   02   01   00   99

To my friend and mentor, Joe Ponterotto, who always saw possibilities where I saw obstacles

and

To my mother, Carmela, for allowing me to experience a world of diversity

CONTENTS

PREFACE

Multicultural counseling has had a dramatic development in the last ten years. The number of journal articles and books dedicated to the topic has been overwhelming, and it is rare to find a graduate curriculum without at least one required course. The development of this field has been so extensive that one can trace a multiplicity of viewpoints and even begin to talk about different schools within the multicultural movement. More recently, the pervasiveness of multiculturalism in counseling has provoked a reaction from those who say that such emphasis on the culture-specific has led us to forget about similarities among all human beings as well as universal counseling principles.

The present text contributes to this ongoing dialogue by developing a situational-hierarchical approach to multicultural counseling. It is intended for professors, students, and practitioners of counseling who wish to understand how multiculturalism can be integrated into each counseling modality. This book's uniqueness lies in the integration and reworking of traditional counseling concepts and principles within the framework of multiculturalism. It contains some fundamental constructs in multicultural counseling, offers an overview of basic concepts relevant to a particular counseling modality, and, through the use of lengthy case examples, demonstrates the dynamic integration of multiculturalism in counseling.

Chapter 1 deals with current controversies as it presents the different schools emerging in multicultural counseling and traces their historical development. I develop my own viewpoint and theoretical exposition, termed "situational-hierarchical theory."

Chapters 2 and 3 lay the theoretical groundwork for the book, and they deal with two fundamental constructs in multicultural counseling: second-culture acquisition theory and cultural identity development theory. Chapter 2 deals with the various behavioral forms, the result of cognitive and emotional processes that individuals can assume when in contact with a culture different than their own. Chapter 3 examines cultural identity development theory and describes the various stages or statuses that individuals pass through in terms of how they relate to their own culture. Chapter 3 concludes Part I of the book, the historical and theoretical setting for multicultural counseling.

Part II is much more applied and attempts to integrate the theories of second-culture acquisition and cultural identity development with some traditional constructs in counseling. This integrationist approach reflects my own viewpoint that there are some traditional principles and strategies that, if used in conjunction with a multicultural perspective, can be useful in serving diverse populations. Part II is organized around counseling modality: Chapter 4 deals with individual multicultural counseling; Chapter 5 with groups; Chapter 6 with families; and Chapter 7 with organizations. Each of these chapters follows a similar format. They begin with some traditional principles relevant to the particular modality, followed by a critique and integration of said principles within a multicultural perspective, and ending with a lengthy case example applying what has been discussed in earlier parts of the chapter. Chapter 8 concludes the book by revisiting the etic versus emic debate, the challenge posed by constructivism, and the integration of psychodynamic principles with multicultural counseling.

This format is intended to accomplish a number of purposes. First, it attempts to portray multicultural counseling as a dynamic perspective from which to approach each and every relationship and by which to determine the importance of cultural factors within a particular situation. Rather than seeing multiculturalism as one way of working alongside many others or one theory to choose from among many others, this book projects multiculturalism as a pervasive factor to be reckoned with on a constant basis. Therein lies a second purpose of the format: to show how multiculturalism can be infused into various dimensions of a curriculum rather than serving as the beginning and ending of the required course. Too often, faculty feel exempt from dealing with issues of multiculturalism in their respective courses, alluding to the fact there exists a required course for dealing with such matters. This compartmentalizing of multiculturalism in counseling cannot be reconciled with our own position of seeing cultural factors as ubiquitous.

As a result of understanding multiculturalism as a dynamic and pervasive factor in counseling, this book can fit into a counseling curriculum in several ways. Most introduction to counseling texts dedicate chapters to different counseling modalities (individual, group, family, etc.) and most likely will include a chapter on multicultural counseling. This text, if used in an introduction to counseling course, would provide a unique and fresh approach to counseling. Multiculturalism in counseling would be treated as primary, with different counseling modalities reviewed in their traditional approaches and integrated into a multicultural perspective. This avoids understanding multiculturalism as a new approach viewed alongside traditional approaches. Rather, traditional approaches are examined, reviewed, and refined through the lens of multiculturalism. There has been a lot of emphasis in recent years among those who are training counselors that this should be the approach to multicultural counseling. I hope that the structure and format of this text will enable counseling professors to introduce their students to counseling through multiculturalism—rather than the reverse.

A second way this text could fit into the counseling curriculum is within a graduate course on multicultural counseling. Though the first section of the book (fundamental constructs) might parallel other books on multicultural counseling, the second section, rather than dedicating chapters to a diverse group, deals with different counseling modalities through a multicultural perspective. This would allow students to understand how multiculturalism can be a part of different counseling modalities, while at the same time introducing them to some fundamental principles relevant to each modality. Should the counselor-educator use this text in conjunction with one that treats counseling issues specific to various minority groups, I believe this combination would provide a comprehensive treatment of multiculturalism in counseling. Therefore, I hope that both practitioners and educators find this book useful—practitioners who wish to incorporate a dynamic multicultural perspective into their work and educators who wish to show how multiculturalism can be infused throughout the counseling curriculum. As the number of books dedicated to multicultural counseling continues to grow, I believe it is important for professionals in the field to allow for a multiplicity of viewpoints and approaches to this most important topic. I hope this book is considered in that vein, and I welcome the comments and feedback of readers as we struggle to understand ourselves in relation to others, and most especially others who are culturally different.

ACKNOWLEDGMENTS

Writing my first book and being its sole author created in me an undercurrent of insecurity and doubt. Without the support of many, I would have become overwhelmed and paralyzed by such feelings. I want to recognize those who lent a helping hand in preventing that.

First, I wish to acknowledge Peacock Publishers for giving me the opportunity to write this book. Most especially, I wish to thank Dick Welna for his constant guidance, support, and reinforcement, and Steve Gold, whose visit in May of 1996 made it all possible. Without their trust in me, this book would still be in the world of ideas.

Also, thanks to John Beasley for being such a helpful and supportive manuscript editor, and thanks to my colleague, Eugene Bartoo, for his support and understanding as I struggled through parts of the manuscript.

Thanks to my friends and colleagues, Buddy Gushue and George Simon, for reading parts of the manuscript and offering invaluable suggestions. Thanks also to my niece, Kelly, and my nephew, Brett, whose childhood wonder and interest in my book inspired me to keep writing, and to Eleanor, whose guidance and intellect always challenged me to grow as a writer.

Finally, I wish to thank the people of the countries where I have visited and lived over the years. Without these experiences, I would not have understood the richness of sharing with those different than myself. Most especially I am grateful to the people of Puerto Rico, Dominican Republic, Spain, Haiti, Nigeria, and South Africa. A final note of thanks to my sisters and brothers of the South Bronx, whose generosity and love taught me to believe that a true multicultural society can be more than just a dream.

PART I

—◦⟋⟍◦—

Fundamentals in Multicultural Counseling

Part I contains the historical and theoretical foundation chapters of *Multiculturalism in Counseling*. Chapter 1 traces the development of the field and outlines the various viewpoints and controversies existing at the present moment. More specifically, Chapter 1 deals with the etic versus emic debate, the various typologies of multicultural counseling, and the understanding of culture as worldview.

Chapter 2 is dedicated to the theoretical construct of second-culture acquisition. The processes that individuals undergo when two different cultures come into contact, along with the various forms of cultural adaptation, are discussed at length. The chapter considers biculturalism as the richest and most highly developed form of cultural adaptation. It also covers measures of acculturation critically and emphasizes a bidirectional over a linear approach to such measures.

Chapter 3 deals with racial/cultural identity development theory and explains the various models involving minorities, Blacks, and Whites. Competing models are examined, along with a discussion of the challenges created by the various measures of racial/cultural identity development. Part I provides the theoretical framework for multiculturalism in counseling and prepares the reader for the applied integration of this theory presented in Part II.

—◦◦◦—

CHAPTER 1

MULTICULTURALISM IN COUNSELING

THE EVOLVING FIELD OF MULTICULTURAL COUNSELING

Multicultural counseling is counseling that takes place among people of different cultural backgrounds (Jackson, 1995). Some authors have wanted to make a distinction between multicultural and cross-cultural counseling, with the former reserved for when cultural/contextual factors are integrated into all phases of the counseling process. However, this book follows the more conventional path of using the two terms interchangeably and in the broad sense includes, in addition to racial and ethnic differences, sexual orientation, socioeconomic class, ability, and age (Atkinson, Morton, & Sue, 1998).

From the early 1980s to the present day, there has been an exceptional rise in the professional literature dedicated to multicultural counseling. With such movement, it becomes possible to trace the development of multicultural counseling as more contemporary works have built upon, and even deviated from, early approaches.

Early Contributions

Early multicultural counseling criticized the appropriateness of traditional theories and techniques as emanating from a male, White, Eurocentric perspective and emphasized the need for interventions sensitive to clients from nondominant cultural backgrounds.[1] Some of the pioneers in raising the consciousness of cultural encapsulation among counseling professionals were Pederson, Lonner, and Draguns (1976), Sue and Sue (1971), and Vontress (1971). As a result of this early sensitivity, a profusion of books began to emerge during the 1980s on the topic of multicultural counseling (Atkinson, Morton, & Sue, 1998; Ho, 1987; Marsella & Pederson, 1981; McGoldrick, Pearce, & Giordano, 1982; Pederson, 1985, 1988; Powell, Yamamoto, Romero, & Morales, 1983; Sue, 1981; Vacc, Wittmer, & DeVaney, 1988). Many of these books and others had the same semiencyclopedic format—a first part that introduced the reader to the field of multiculturalism in counseling and a second part that dedicated a chapter to different underrepresented groups. These latter chapters would follow a similar format—introducing the reader historically and psychosocially to the group under study and ending with recommended interventions for that particular group. Books of this type served a laudable purpose in challenging counselors to use more culturally sensitive interventions.

However, there was a dual risk inherent in works of this type: First, they tended to ignore intragroup differences, leading to overgeneralization and stereotyping of minority groups; and secondly, they placed an emphasis upon technique in helping the counselor to work more effectively with diverse clients. This emphasis led in some instances to a "one size fits all" approach to intervening on behalf of the culturally different.

---

[1] The terms "dominant" and "nondominant" are used throughout this book to contrast cultural groupings based on political, economic, and social power. Nondominant groups share unequally in the power structure of society and therefore are given the status of "minority." Some examples of dominant versus nondominant groupings are: White versus Black; male versus female; and heterosexual versus homosexual.

Intergroup Versus Intragroup Differences

As a result of the just described concerns, there began to emerge in the mid-1980s a sensitivity to intragroup (within group) differences among minority groups, whereas the early emphasis in multicultural counseling appeared to be on intergroup (between group) differences. Counselors working cross-culturally were now being challenged to know two things about a client: What are the broad cultural patterns of the client's salient referent group (intergroup/intercultural difference), and to what *extent* is this particular client representative of such patterns (intragroup/intracultural difference) (Gushue, 1993; Gushue & Sciarra, 1995)?

To help examine intragroup differences, the counseling field has relied upon two very important paradigms: second-culture acquisition and cultural identity development, which form respectively Chapters 2 and 3 of this book. While the encyclopedic approach can help with intergroup differences, the use of constructs such as second-culture acquisition and cultural identity development help to avoid the cookbook approach (Speight, Myers, Cox, & Highlen, 1991) to multicultural counseling. Speight et al. (1991) rightly pointed out that the difference between these so-called cookbooks and stereotyping is not always clear, and Sue and Zane (1987) warn about applying culture-specific techniques without considering the appropriateness of such techniques for a particular client from a diverse culture.

In debunking the role of the counselor as a "chameleon of technique"(Patterson, 1996), the concept of the counselor as collaborator with the client (Egan, 1998) in helping to design a more workable fit between dominant and nondominant culture has begun to emerge. The idea of counselor and client as cocreators of a more workable cultural narrative has important implications for counselor awareness. Since most counselors are from a Eurocentric background and are therefore representative of the dominant culture, it became imperative for them to be aware of their own cultural biases, imprinting, and identity development and to examine how these come into play in working with diverse clients. For this precise reason, Chapter 3 of this book dedicates substantial space to White racial identity development where "White" is a metaphor for the dominant culture. New directions in multicultural counseling are toward increased understanding of the process that counselor and counselee go through in developing greater awareness of their own cultural identities, and how these might either facilitate or obfuscate the counseling process.

Constructivism and Multiculturalism

Facilitating this return to personal qualities of the counselor (Patterson, 1996), rather than relying on an aggregation of techniques to serve the ever-increasing number of diverse groups in our society, has been the constructivist movement in counseling and psychotherapy (Gergen & Gergen, 1991; Gonzalez, Biever, & Gardner, 1994; Guba & Lincoln, 1989; Neimeyer & Mahoney, 1995). It is beyond the scope of this chapter to give an in-depth, comprehensive treatment of constructivism, but its connection with multiculturalism and the apparent disregard for this connection in the literature are worth examining.

Constructivism has its roots in the German idealist/interpretivist tradition perhaps most associated with Wilhelm Dilthey, who introduced the concept of *hermeneutics*. For Dilthey (1954, 1977), understanding of another must access the *meaning* associated with a particular action, and meaning must be understood within context. This knowledge of the context or background for proper interpretation of another is what Dilthey meant by hermeneutics; and the notion of hermeneutics gave rise to the interpretivist paradigm in social science research (Schwandt, 1994). The social scientist must interpret (understand) the other within context, within the group or culture in which the other functions. Today, the term *constructivism* seems to be preferred over interpretivism, though many writers acknowledge that constructivist, interpretive, and hermeneutical are all similar notions (Guba & Lincoln, 1989; Schwandt, 1994). They share in common the idea that reality is basically a construction of the individual mind; these constructions are the result of the meanings individuals give (construct) for their experiences; human beings act toward things on the basis of these meanings (Woods, 1992); and the constructions of the investigator cannot be (and should not be) separated from those of the investigated (Schwandt, 1994). In social constructionism, the focus is more on the mutually agreed-upon meanings of a particular group and their role in shaping individual constructions (Berger & Luckmann, 1966; Gergen & Gergen, 1991; Guba & Lincoln, 1989; Schwandt, 1994).

The contructivist paradigm can help to explain further a multicultural approach to counseling. If meaning given to experience is what determines human action, and meanings vary across individuals and groups, astute multicultural counselors will see their primary task as accessing and understanding the meaning clients give to their experiences. Often clients from diverse cultures will attach meanings to events and experiences that are quite different than the counselor's own meanings and interpretations for the very same event.

Let's take, for example, a Latino client in counseling who begins to hear voices in his head telling him to do harmful things. The counselor immediately begins to give meaning to such an event as a psychosis, perhaps indicative of a schizophrenic break, and wants a psychiatric evaluation. The client, on the other hand, says hearing voices means he is possessed by an evil spirit and wants to go to an *espiritista* to exorcise the evil spirits, thus allowing the good spirit to reenter his body. Whose story is better? More correct? More valid? More true?

From a constructivist/multicultural viewpoint, these are misguided questions. The multicultural counselor understands that there are multiple truths, meanings, and constructions, and that counseling is "*not the vindication of one story over another nor the replacement of one story with another*" (Pare, 1996, p. 38). Rather, counseling is a collaborative effort in coconstructing alternate meanings and stories to provide a more workable fit or greater cultural harmony with the client's experience. Returning to our example, a decision can be made to include the espiritista as a collaborator in the healing process of the client in conjunction with pharmacological therapy. The counselor may come to understand that there is something evil about hearing a voice mandating harm to oneself or to another. The client, on the other hand, may come to understand this evil can have different causes and does not mean that he or she is an evil person. Multicultural counseling becomes an "intercultural give and take, a respectful exchange of meanings, a negotiation toward harmony between diverse stories" (Pare, 1996, p. 37).

From Melting Pot to Mosaic

Speight et al. (1991) made reference to the yin-yang theory of Eastern philosophies, which talks about a harmony of differences. It evokes images of a mosaic and a mesh in which a picture assumes beauty because of the togetherness of different identities that remain separate (diverse), yet form a part of the whole (integrated). If multiculturalism is a gift to be enjoyed, one is not eager to look for sameness in order to achieve a sense of security; one learns to be secure with differences. Critics of multiculturalism maintain that an emphasis upon differences blurs the sameness we all share, and it is our shared sameness that builds a solid foundation for the counseling relationship. However, past experience has taught us that the emphasis upon shared sameness has led to the "melting pot" metaphor for American society. Cultural differences are erased ("melted" down) so as to create a harmonious, look-alike society. Of course, the pot always had a massive amount of White Eurocentrism, resulting in the need for those of different cultural backgrounds to look and act White. Thus, I strongly recommend that the flame be turned off under the melting pot and removed and then be replaced by a mosaic in which harmony and beauty are created not by relinquishing our cultural distinctions but by retaining them. A mosaic understanding implies an attitude that sees differences as multiple opportunities for mutual enrichment. Counselors need not apologize for being enriched culturally by their clients. It's part of the joy and beauty of being a counselor, of entering into a kind of intimacy with another human being—not because they are like me but precisely because they are different.

This approach to multicultural counseling eschews the image of counselor as both expert and having power over the client. The counselor views the encounter first as an opportunity for learning about the client's meaning-making world. The counselor avoids replicating a dynamic found all too often in larger society, where the voices of the dominant culture silence those of nondominant cultures. In multicultural counseling, nondominant voices are not only allowed but given credence, and power is understood as a means for producing a consensus as the counselor works *with* rather than *on* the client (Pare, 1996).

IS ALL COUNSELING MULTICULTURAL?

The emphasis upon the importance of cultural differences and the introduction of constructivism—which views reality as constructed across individuals and groups—raises the question as to whether all counseling is multicultural. Has multicultural counseling just become a politically correct term for emphasizing the differences that exist among individuals and groups? Furthermore, does the emphasis upon differences lead to denial of sameness among human beings, thereby rendering meaningless any general principles of counseling?

Etic Versus Emic Debate

Some critics note that the pendulum has swung too far in the other direction. They agree that the counseling profession for a long time was insensitive to cultural differences and guilty of perpetuating dominant-culture imperialism, but they hasten to add that an overemphasis upon differences ignores the rapidly increasing global interconnectedness of our world (Patterson, 1996); disregards the need for common ground (Pederson, 1996); and fosters an exclusionary, combative, and highly politicized environment (Sue, Ivey, & Pederson, 1996). Pederson (1996) argued that the dichotomy between similarity and difference is a false one in that multicultural counseling must always toe the line between overemphasizing similarity and overemphasizing difference—since the former leads to the melting pot mentality, with prevalence of the dominant group and exploitation of the less powerful (Sue, Ivey, & Pederson, 1996), while the latter leads to stereotyping and a disregard for the need for common ground.

This controversy has been conceptualized as the etic versus emic debate, wherein the former is used to refer to psychological laws along with counseling principles, strategies, and interventions that have universal application as opposed to those that are culture specific (Atkinson, Morton, & Sue, 1998). The etic approach to counseling views the sameness among human beings as greater and more important than their differences (Carter & Qureshi, 1995). The emic approach takes the opposite view. However, the two are not always neatly separated. As an example of how the common ground (the etic) and the culture specific (the emic) are enmeshed, Pederson (1996) offered the establishment of the working alliance. The working alliance, a traditional construct in counseling, is considered an etic factor because of the assumption that no effective counseling, regardless of cultural differences, can take place without a trusting (working) relationship between counselor and counselee. But how that rapport is established effectively will vary from culture to culture. Simply put: The working alliance is an etic factor; the means for establishing it, an emic factor.

To illustrate this point, let's use the clinical example of working with a sociopath. The use of counselor warmth, genuineness, and empathy (characteristics traditionally associated with establishing a working alliance) may only increase the possibility of manipulation by the client. Rather, the counselor establishes the working alliance by confronting any maneuvering and lying and by holding the client responsible for his or her actions. The counselor gains respect by not falling prey to manipulation. In contrast, the establishment of a working alliance with a client grieving the loss of a beloved spouse would require a different approach. The diversity between a grieving spouse and a manipulating sociopath calls for two different strategies. Thus, what is true for these two clinical populations is also true for clients who differ along the lines of cultural rather than clinical variables. For example, the *personalismo* of the Latino culture can require a less formal and more affective counselor, whereas these counselor characteristics may be alienating to some Asian clients. The recognition of all counseling as multicultural to one degree or another does not imply a one-approach-fits-all mentality. Rather, it takes seriously the differences between client and counselor on a host of cultural variables; does not shy away from those differences; and looks to utilize such differences on behalf of the counseling process.

Method Versus Theory

Pederson (1991), in his discussion of multiculturalism as a generic approach to counseling, distinguished between seeing it as a method and as a theory. As method, multiculturalism is a form of analysis, but as theory it "refers to broadly defined social system variables such as ethnographics, demographics, status, and affiliation" (Pederson, 1991, p. 7). Based on our earlier discussion, an emphasis on multiculturalism as method could lead to an overemphasis on technique, whereas multiculturalism as theory leads to understanding oneself and others as a product of cultural variables whose dynamic interaction results in intergroup and intragroup differences. An awareness as to how these variables play out in a counseling relationship constitutes multiculturalism as a generic or ubiquitous (Carter & Qureshi, 1995) approach to counseling. Pederson (1991) rightly indicated that people may change their cultural referent group any number of times during an encounter—moving from race to age to socioeconomic class to religion, and so forth.

Culture, when more broadly defined and understood, should help to remove the "exotic" nature of multiculturalism by appearing not as an obstacle but as a universal construct that helps to gain more accurate understanding of oneself and the client. It is no longer a question of being a universalist (emphasizing sameness) or a multiculturalist (emphasizing diversity) but of understanding multiculturalism as a generic construct. Our shared sameness is that we are all a product of different cultural variables and represents an approach that obviates the peril of minimizing issues of diversity in the counseling relationship. It is not so much finding the middle ground between the etic (universal) approach and the emic (culture-specific) approach to counseling (Speight et al., 1991); nor is it a question of working together in spite of our differences. Rather, the approach can be: We will work together because of our differences. As mentioned earlier, cultural differences may be seen not as an obstacle to overcome, but rather as an opportunity of mutual enrichment for both subjects in the relationship. For the longest time, psychoanalysts have spoken about how their analysands impact them and how their own analysis is constantly in play. Analogously, multicultural counselors allow themselves to impact and be impacted by cultural differences, to enrich and be enriched by such differences, and to elicit carefully and clearly the cultural narrative of the client, thereby evoking the counselor's own cultural narrative. To effectuate this exchange between client and counselor, multicultural counseling makes use of culturally sensitive paradigms such as worldview, second-culture acquisition, and racial/cultural identity development, in lieu of more traditional paradigms emphasizing individuality and intrapsychic development.

Beyond Stereotypes

If one adopts the position that the common ground (the etic) is that we all come from different cultural backgrounds (the emic) that have to be studied and taken seriously, one is not necessarily forced to commit allegiance to one side or the other (Fukuyama, 1990).

Intercultural Versus Intracultural Differences. This common ground of cultural differences is further substantiated by the consideration of both intercultural and intracultural differences (Ho, 1995). An exclusive consideration of the former without the latter leads to the "cookbook" approach to counseling and one size fits all for a cultural grouping. According to Ho (1995), what distinguishes the anthropological concept of culture from the psychological concept is the latter's serious consideration of intracultural differences and not the exclusive attention upon cultural patterns. After informing themselves of cultural patterns, multicultural counselors must then ask: How is this particular person before me both the same and different from his or her cultural group?

It seems rather paradoxical that multicultural awareness would result at times in the very offenses that it was trying to overcome. As mentioned at the beginning of this chapter, early endeavors in the field of multicultural counseling tended to stay at the level of between-group differences. Though we made this point earlier, it deserves repetition. If multicultural counseling is limited to intercultural differences without attending to those that are intracultural, the result will be overgeneralization, stereotyping, and ineffective counseling. Eliminating such monolithic thinking may be the greatest challenge facing multicultural counselors. Cultural categorization without distinction pervades everyday speech, as even professionals talk about "*the* gay population," "*the* Black male," "*the* Native American population," "*the* biracial couple," "*the* disabled," and the list goes on. As an attempt to overcome this tendency, this book uses basically two constructs—cultural identity development and second-culture acquisition—to examine and sensitize counselors to within-group differences. Ho reminded us that culture is both resilient and malleable as cultural traditions survive and persevere over time and are yet "modifiable by both internal and external influences" (Ho, 1995,

p. 12). This dual dynamic of culture as both resilient and malleable will be more fully explored in Chapter 2 on second-culture acquisition.

Transculturalism. The constructs of cultural identity development and second-culture acquisition along with worldview serve to orient the counselor toward having a "transcultural" (Fukuyama, 1990) approach to counseling. Transculturalism is an alternative to understanding multiculturalism as a generic approach to counseling. Fukuyama's (1990) use of the term *transcultural* as an approach to counseling was not meant to imply a moving beyond, or a rising above, culture as the radical constructivists would have us think, but of moving across. It is an invitation to take a cross-cultural journey within our own group, once again trying to emphasize that all counseling is cross-cultural. "Even among members of the same cultural group, no two individuals would be expected to have an identical internalized culture" (Ho, 1995, p. 16). The ability to transcend one's own culture matches one's ability to avoid culturocentrism.

The transcultural journey is a method for increasing self-awareness particular to the cross-cultural counselor. The degree to which counselors are aware of cultural biases operating within themselves is the degree to which they can be sensitive cross-cultural counselors. Once again, we return to the traditional adage regarding counseling: "Counselor, know thyself." In short, counselors need to explore their own as well as their clients' internalized culture. Ho (1995) went even further to indicate that a cross-cultural journey "may be taken within a single bienculturated mind" (p. 15). Thus, the two traditional counseling terms of *interpersonal* (between two or more people) and *intrapersonal* (within oneself) have their analogues in multicultural counseling. Counselor and client may look at culture crossing between themselves (interpersonal) and within themselves (intrapersonal).

A Tridimensional Approach. Ho's (1995) concept of internalized culture posed a striking similarity to Ibrahim's (1985, 1991) concept of worldview. Ibrahim suggests a tridimensional model for working cross-culturally composed of the majority culture, the client's subculture, and the client's worldview. According to Ibrahim, having an encyclopedic knowledge of the client's subculture is helpful but not enough for effective cross-cultural counseling. The counselor must also consider an analysis of the client's "subjective reality, how this may overlap with his or her primary culture, and the place this subjective reality has in the larger culture" (Ibrahim, 1985, p. 630). When Ibrahim talks about subjective reality, the reader cannot help but consider Ho's (1995) notion of internalized culture within the same vein. Also, like Ho, Ibrahim emphasized the need for counselors to be aware of their own worldview before they can understand, accept, and work within the worldview of the client. Absolute objectivity on the part of the counselor is neither required nor possible, as such objectivity is perhaps an artifact of traditional psychoanalysis. On the contrary, multicultural counselors are aware of how their subjective worldview (or internalized culture) is interfacing with that of the client's by identifying the similarities and differences between their meaning-making worlds. In multicultural counseling, the collaboration between counselor and client takes the form of the counselor's considerations of the client as a cultural equal (Ibrahim, 1985), yet different. The working alliance should be built upon this premise in multicultural counseling.

TOWARD A THEORY OF MULTICULTURAL COUNSELING

Up to this point, we have discussed multiculturalism as a generic approach to counseling and have also alluded to the danger that such an approach poses in relativizing cultural differences. In other words, if we are all culturally different, are all cultural differences to be accorded the same degree of importance?

A Typology of Multicultural Counseling

Carter and Qureshi (1995) offered a typology of approaches to multicultural counseling that can begin to generate an answer to the relative importance of cultural differences. They classify five various approaches to cross-cultural training: universal, ubiquitous, traditional, race-based, and pan-national.

Universal. The universal approach emphasizes transcending culture and focusing on the similarities among human beings. "On this basis, then, we are first and foremost human beings, and only secondarily does our experience and identity derive from other reference groups (e.g., ethnicity, race, gender)" (Carter & Qureshi, 1995, p. 245). The universal approach does not deny cultural differences but clearly sees them as secondary to similarities among human beings. It is synonymous with the formerly discussed etic approach to counseling.

Ubiquitous. This approach celebrates cultural differences and recognizes them as multiple and situationally determined. Unlike the universal approach, it does not view cultural differences as secondary. It is the approach taken by Pederson (1991) when he talks about multicultural counseling as both a fourth force and a generic approach to counseling. As does Ho (1995), the ubiquitous approach holds that an encounter between any two human beings is to be considered cross-cultural since any two human beings will bring together, on one or more levels, a difference in cultural background.

Traditional. This approach approximates the early endeavors in multicultural counseling in that culture is understood as common experience in the functions of socialization and environment. Consequently, the effective multicultural counselor would access knowledge of the other's culture, thus establishing the basis of empathy. The traditional approach does not consider the dynamics of dominant versus nondominant cultures.

Race-Based. If one were to assume the position that race superimposes itself upon all other cultural variables at all times, this would be classified as the "race-based" approach to multiculturalism, according to the Carter and Qureshi (1995) typology. The authors advance the idea that the race-based approach is the only one that takes into serious consideration the difference-of-power dynamics among cultural groupings. Race is the one variable that is neither fluid nor flexible, as it is determined by skin color and physical characteristics, and upon these very visible characteristics "historically ingrained ideas and assumptions about one's place in society begin to be applied" (Carter & Qureshi, 1995, p. 252).

The race-based approach affords a category for approaching multicultural counseling where one and only one cultural variable is superimposed upon all others, namely that of race. However, if one believes there is another such variable—gender, for example—it would achieve categorical status. A gender-based approach to counseling would recognize gender and not race as the superimposed variable since it, too, is determined by physical characteristics upon which ideas and assumptions about one's place in society are applied. The debate will continue as to whether race supersedes gender or vice versa. A good example of this debate has been the women's movement urged on by a gender-based worldview, yet criticized for not being sensitized to Black women's distinctive place in society.

Pan-National. This is an expansion of the race-based approach to global proportions. Whereas the former is primarily concerned with the dynamics of racial group membership in the United States, the pan-national approach also sees race as definitive of culture, but in broader terms of European culture seen as a force antithetical and oppressive to those from less-dominant cultures. The pan-national approach is rooted in the psychology of oppression and therefore views counseling as essential to liberating the counselee, which in turn will also liberate counselors from their identification with an oppressive culture.

The above typology helps to clarify some of the different approaches to multiculturalism in counseling and lays the foundation for articulating my own approach.

A Situational-Hierarchical Position of Multicultural Counseling

If one were to assume the ubiquitous approach to multicultural counseling, would it follow that all cultural differences are to be given the same degree of importance? The answer to this question is a categorical "no." One cannot relativize the cultural differences across all groups. For example, cultural differences based on geographical location (a White Northerner and a White Southerner) are not to be accorded the same significance as differences based on a Black person living in a predominantly White society. However, race also can be situational. For a Black person living in a predominantly Black country, other cultural variables might assume greater importance than that of race. Given the sociopolitical history of racism against non-Whites, the cultural significance of being non-White has to be distinguished hierarchically on the scale of cultural variables. It is important to highlight that, although this book takes what might be called the ubiquitous approach to multicultural counseling, it also incorporates a situational-hierarchical scale of cultural variables. Situational because, in any one particular counseling situation, certain cultural variables will assume more or less importance. Hierarchical because, given the history of oppression against certain groups (e.g., Blacks and women), membership in these groups must be recognized as having greater input than membership in others.

The situational-hierarchical approach to multicultural counseling combines the underpinnings of both the ubiquitous and race-based approaches to multicultural counseling. Like the ubiquitous approach, the situational-hierarchical approach takes seriously human differences in the counseling relationship and considers these differences to be cultural. Like the race-based approach, it does not accord cultural groupings and identities the same level of significance (the hierarchical dimension). Going through life as a White or a Black person will determine much more psychologically, socially, and politically than, let's say, going through life as a Baptist or a Catholic. In a Black and White counseling dyad, racial difference is superimposed upon other cultural differences. However, unlike the race-based approach, the situational-hierarchical model considers the possibility that there are times (situations) in counseling when race may not be the superimposed cultural variable. Take for example, a Black woman at a predominantly Black college who comes to the counseling center because of problems with her roommate who is also Black. The client is from a very poor family in the inner city as opposed to her roommate, whose father is a very successful Black businessman. The client feels her roommate is constantly making disparaging remarks about their difference in social class. In this counseling situation, the culture of socioeconomic class would seem to superimpose itself upon race. For the counselor in this situation to insist that being Black rather than being poor is the "real" issue may be missing the mark.

In dealing with the construct of cultural identity development, the reference is to one's psychological response to whatever cultural variable is occupying primary psychological space. Thus, the preference is to talk about cultural identity development rather than racial identity development in order to encompass the multitudinal dimensions of multicultural counseling. However, I do not wish to imply that in talking about cultural identity development we are putting racial identity on an equal plain with other cultural identities. The psychological response to being non-White will assume more energy than will the response to other identities.

This hierarchy can be expanded to look at other cultural variables, particularly that of gender. The race-based theorists would argue that gender ought not be given the same prominence as race. The feminists might argue differently and want gender to be seen as the superimposed cultural variable. Though this book agrees with the race-based theorists to an extent ("to an extent" because the model is situational and hierarchical), the belief is that there are situations in which gender might be superimposed upon race. Let's take for example a workplace in which a racially diverse group of women are struggling for equal pay with their male counterparts. In this situation, the discrimination may be more along the lines of gender rather than race. Gender identity, *in this particular situation*, may evoke a greater psychological response, occupy more psychological space, and consume more psychological energy. On the other hand, it would be erroneous on the part of the White women to assume that because they are all women they will be treated equally. In simple terms, the White women in this particular scenario would have to recognize the dual oppression of their non-White counterparts. In short, this book espouses the belief that the ubiquitous and race-based approaches to multicultural counseling need not be exclusive and can be reconciled through a situational-hierarchical theory of cultural variability.

TOWARD A DEFINITION OF CULTURE

Perhaps readers find themselves a bit frustrated at this point because of our refusal to offer a categorical definition of what is meant by the term *culture*.

The previous pages of this first chapter have played descriptively as opposed to theoretically with the term. Jackson and Meadows (1991) indicated that, for counselors to work effectively across cultures, they need a clear understanding of the term culture. According to Bennett (1990), prior to the 1950s, culture was defined in terms of patterns of behavior and customs, with the focus on the observable aspects of culture (dress, food, and music). These observable behaviors, however, are manifestations of deeper, unacknowledged levels of culture. According to Jackson and Meadows (1991), the 1960s saw an emphasis on ethnographic variables (nationality, ethnicity, shared history) for distinguishing cultural groups. However, this "ethnic" identification appeared to belong only to people of color. In order to obviate this exclusiveness, Pederson (1988) proposed a social systems approach to culture including demographic, status, affiliation, and ethnographic variables—thus allowing no one to be exempt from cross-cultural reflection. Other definitions of culture focused on shared values (White, 1975) and shared knowledge and belief systems (Spradley & McCurdy, 1975). Carter and Qureshi (1995) wrote that "for most scholars, culture is a learned system of meaning and behavior that is passed from one generation to the next" (p. 241).

Culture as Worldview

It was Tirandis (1975) who introduced the notion of culture as shared worldview understood as presuppositions and assumptions that individuals hold about the makeup of their world. Jackson and Meadows (1991), building on the concept of worldview, talked about "deep culture," which they defined as philosophical assumptions having to do with ontology (the nature of reality), cosmology (the order and arrangement of reality), epistemology (the nature of knowledge), axiology (the nature of values by which people live), logic (the nature of reasoning and systematic inquiry), and process (the particular method of operation or functioning). Ibrahim (1991) wrote: "Without the worldview as a mediating variable, both knowledge of specific cultures and culture-specific techniques can be misapplied, leading to charges of ethical violation and cultural oppression. Once the worldview (of the counselor, client, educator, trainer, or student) is clearly understood, appropriate applications of theory and research can take place" (p. 14). The mandate to clearly understand the worldview of oneself and another would appear to be a daunting and perhaps lifelong task. Nevertheless, the concept of worldview does help to make counseling more client specific and avoid the "one size fits all" mentality. Ibrahim (1991) linked worldview to cultural identities (ethnicity, gender, age, lifestage, socioeconomic status, education, religion, philosophy of life, beliefs, values, and assumptions). The Scale to Assess Worldviews (Ibrahim & Kahn, 1987; Ibrahim & Owen, 1994) was developed to measure one's view of:

1. Human nature as good, bad, or a combination of good and bad;

2. Social relationships as lineal-hierarchical, collateral-mutual, and individualistic;

3. Nature as something to be subjugated and controlled, to be lived in harmony with, or to be accepted as having control over people;

4. Time as past, present, and future; and

5. Activity as being, being-in-becoming, and doing.

Ibrahim (1991) continued to say: "[T]he worldview construct and theory provide information regarding how well the client fits or does not fit the values, beliefs, and assumptions of his or her primary group. It also assists one in developing an understanding of how the worldview of the larger society has been assimilated by the client providing a measure of acculturation" (p. 15). When different worldviews come into contact, issues of second-culture acquisition arise. Chapter 2 is dedicated to this very important topic.

Trevino (1996) discussed the issue of worldview and how it should relate to change in the multicultural counseling process. She also raised the question of whether change is about changing the client's worldview or working within the worldview of the client. Trevino suggested that the answer to this question lies in conceptualizing worldview as a mediating variable: "[T]here is a significant body of research suggesting that congruency between counselor and client enhances the therapeutic relationship, whereas discrepancy between the two facilitates change" (Trevino, 1996, p. 203). The concern ought to be not that two worldviews are different but whether the coming together, the interaction of these worldviews, can be therapeutic. A fundamental assumption of this book is that differences in worldview increase the possibility of exploring alternative perspectives and solutions by fomenting more divergent thinking.

SUMMARY

The chapter began by exploring the changing face of multicultural counseling supported by an invitation to abandon the melting pot metaphor of North American society in favor of a mosaic. The need for accentuating intragroup as well as intergroup differences to avoid stereotyping and overgeneralization was highlighted. An attempt was made to reconcile the etic versus the emic by considering the common ground to be our cultural differences. Finally, a situational-hierarchical approach to multicultural counseling was advanced to avoid considering all cultural differences equally significant.

With the unprecedented growth in the last 10 to 15 years of professional literature dedicated to multicultural counseling, it is next to impossible in an introductory book chapter to apprise the reader of all approaches to multicultural counseling. Thus, my intention has not been a thorough review of the literature but to select certain contemporary issues in multicultural counseling as groundwork for the following chapters. If a strong enough case has been made for considering both between-group and within-group differences, the reader then is prepared to appreciate the next two chapters. Chapters 2, Second-Culture Acquisition, and 3, Cultural Identity Development, are paradigmatic tools designed to facilitate consideration and understanding of within-group differences of culturally diverse clients. Upon reflection, there appear numerous theoretical frameworks and methods for multicultural counseling. A counselor who is seriously interested in multiculturalism will not lack opportunities for professional development. However, there is no book, article, workshop, or conference that can create an effective multicultural counselor. Effective multicultural counseling ultimately stems from embracing a particular way of being in the world, of viewing diversity as a necessary and beautiful part of creation, and of wanting to hear the all-too-often silenced voices of underrepresented groups.

REFERENCES

Atkinson, D.R., Morton, G., & Sue, D.W. (1998). *Counseling American minorities.* (5th ed.) Boston: McGraw-Hill.

Bennett, C. (Ed.). (1990). *Comprehensive multicultural education.* Boston: Allyn & Bacon.

Berger, P., & Luckmann, T. (1966). *The social construct of reality.* Garden City, NY: Anchor.

Carter, R.T., & Qureshi, A. (1995). A typology of philosophical assumptions in multi-cultural counseling and training. In J.G. Ponterotto, J.M. Casas, L.A. Suzuki, & C.M. Alexander (Eds.), *Handbook of multicultural counseling* (pp. 239–262). Thousand Oaks, CA: Sage.

Dilthey, W. (1954). *The essence of philosophy* (S.A. Emery & W.T. Emery, Trans.). Chapel Hill: University of North Carolina Press.

Dilthey, W. (1977). *Descriptive psychology and historical understanding* (R.M. Zaner & K.L. Heiges, Trans.). The Hague: Nijhoff.

Egan, G. (1998). *The skilled helper.* (6th ed.) Pacific Grove, CA: Brooks/Cole.

Fukuyama, M.A. (1990). Taking a universal approach to multicultural counseling. *Counselor Education and Supervision, 30,* 6–17.

Gergen, K.J., & Gergen, M.M. (1991). Toward reflexive methodologies. In F. Steier (Ed.), *Research and reflexivity* (pp. 76–95). Newbury Park, CA: Sage.

Gonzalez, R.C., Biever, J.L., & Gardner, G.T. (1994). The multicultural perspective in therapy: A social constructionist approach. *Psychotherapy, 31,* 515–524.

Guba, E.G., & Lincoln, Y.S. (1989). *Fourth generation evaluation.* Newbury Park, CA: Sage.

Gushue, G.V., (1993). Cultural identity development and family assessment: An inter-action model. *The Counseling Psychologist, 21,* 487–513.

Gushue, G.V, & Sciarra, D.T. (1995). Culture and families. In J.G. Ponterotto, J.M. Casas, L.A. Suzuki, & C.M. Alexander (Eds.), *Handbook of multicultural counseling* (pp. 586–606). Thousand Oaks, CA: Sage.

Ho, D.Y. (1995). Internalized culture, culturocentrism, and transcendence. *The Counseling Psychologist, 23,* 4–24.

Ho, M.K. (1987). *Family therapy with ethnic minorities.* Newbury Park, CA: Sage.

Ibrahim, F.A. (1985). Effective cross-cultural counseling and psychotherapy: A frame-work. *The Counseling Psychologist, 13,* 625–638.

Ibrahim, F.A. (1991). Contribution of cultural worldview to generic counseling and de-velopment. *Journal of Counseling and Development, 70,* 13–19.

Ibrahim, F.A., & Kahn, H. (1987). Assessment of worldviews. *Psychological Reports, 60,* 163–176.

Ibrahim, F.A., & Owen, S.V. (1994). Factor analytic structure of the Scale to Assess World View. *Current Psychology: Developmental-Learning-Personality-Social, 13,* 201–209.

Jackson, A.P., Meadows, F.B. (1991). Getting to the bottom to understand the top. *Journal of Counseling and Development, 70,* 72–76.

Jackson, M.L. (1995). Multicultural counseling: Historical perspectives. In J.G. Ponterotto, J.M. Casas, L.A. Suzuki, & C.M. Alexander (Eds.), *Handbook of multicultural counseling* (pp. 3–16). Thousand Oaks, CA: Sage.

Marsella, A.J., & Pederson, P.B. (1981). *Cross cultural counseling and psychotherapy.* New York: Pergamon Press.

McGoldrick, M., Pearce, J., & Giordano, J. (1982). *Ethnicity and family therapy.* New York: Guilford Press.

Neimeyer, R.A., & Mahoney, M.J. (1995). *Constructivism in psychotherapy.* Washington, DC: American Psychological Association.

Pare, D.A. (1996). Culture and meaning: Expanding the metaphorical repertoire of family therapy. *Family Process, 35,* 21–42.

Patterson, C.H. (1996). Multicultural counseling: From diversity to universality. *Journal of Counseling and Development, 74,* 227–235.

Pederson, P. (1985). *Handbook of cross cultural counseling and therapy.* Westport, CT: Greenwood.

Pederson, P. (1988). *A handbook for developing multicultural awareness.* Alexandria, VA: American Association for Counseling and Development.

Pederson, P. (1991). Multiculturalism as a generic approach to counseling. *Journal of Counseling and Development, 70,* 6–12.

Pederson, P. (1996). The importance of both similarities and differences in multicultural counseling: Reaction to Patterson. *Journal of Counseling and Development, 74,* 236–237.

Pederson, P., Lonner, W.J., & Draguns, J.G. (1976). *Counseling across cultures.* Honolulu: University of Hawaii Press.

Powell, G.J., Yamamoto, J., Romero, A., & Morales, K.A. (1983). *The psychosocial development of minority group children.* New York: Brunner/Mazel.

Schwandt, T.A. (1994). Contructivist, interpretivist approaches to human inquiry. In N.K. Denzin & Y. S. Lincoln (Eds.), *Handbook of qualitative research* (pp. 118–137). Thousand Oaks, CA: Sage.

Speight, S.L., Myers, L.J., Cox, C.I., & Highlen, P.S. (1991). A redefinition of multicultural counseling. *Journal of Counseling and Development, 70,* 29–36.

Spradley, J., & McCurdy, D. (1975). *Anthropology: The cultural perspective.* New York: Wiley.

Sue, D.W. (1981). *Counseling the culturally different: Theory and practice.* New York: Wiley.

Sue, D.W., Ivey, A.E., & Pederson, P.B. (1996). *A theory of multicultural counseling and therapy.* Pacific Grove, CA: Brooks/Cole.

Sue, S., & Sue, D.W. (1971). Chinese-American personality and mental health. *Amerasia Journal, 2,* 39–49.

Sue, S., & Zane, N. (1987). The role of culture and cultural techniques in psychotherapy: A critique and reformulation. *American Psychologist, 42,* 37–45.

Tirandis, H.C. (1975). Culture training, cognitive complexity, and interpersonal attitudes. In R. Brislin, S. Bochner, & W. Lonner (Eds.), *Cross cultural perspectives on learning* (pp. 39–77). New York: Halsted.

. (1996). Worldview and change in cross cultural counseling. *The Counseling Psychologist, 24,* 198–215.

Vacc, N.A., Wittmer, J., DeVaney, S. (1988). *Experiencing and counseling multicultural and diverse populations.* Muncie, IN: Accelerated Development.

Vontress, C.E. (1971). *Counseling Negroes: Series 6. Minority groups and guidance.* Boston: Houghton Mifflin.

White, L. (1975). *The concept of cultural systems: A key to understanding tribes and nations.* New York: Columbia University Press.

Woods, P. (1992). Symbolic interactionism: Theory and method. In M.D. LeCompte, W.D. Millnoy, & J. Preissle (Eds.), *The handbook of qualitative research* (pp. 337–404). San Diego: Academic Press.

—⟋⟋⟋—

CHAPTER 2

THE SECOND-CULTURE ACQUISITION PROCESS

When two different cultures come into contact, be they individuals or groups, a process of adaptation is unleashed. The precise form of this adaptation and the amount of anxiety or stress associated with it depend on many variables, which we will explore in this chapter. Counselors working with clients from nondominant cultural backgrounds need to assess their acculturative form and the amount of stress resulting from living in a different environment.

VARIETIES OF CULTURAL ADAPTATION

Cultural adaptation can be defined as the way individuals choose to deal with living in a dominant culture that is different than their own. Berry (1980) conceived of the "other culture" as a stimulus that evokes a reaction of either moving toward, moving against, or moving away. "Moving toward" assumes that a positive relationship to the dominant culture is sought. More recently, the adaptation process has been categorized as either unidirectional, bidirectional, or multidirectional. Unidirectional implies that one adapts by moving in a single direction toward one culture and away from another. In contrast, bidirectional adaptation implies a moving back and forth between two cultures, allowing the individual to feel at home in both. Multidirectionality implies that individuals, while maintaining a positive identity with their culture of origin, are capable of participating in various and complex societal structures made up of multiple cultural groupings (LaFromboise, Coleman, & Gerton, 1993). Following are various forms of cultural adaptation that are either unidirectional, bidirectional, or multidirectional.

Assimilation

Traditionally in the United States, establishment of a positive relationship with the dominant culture has resulted in a process of *assimilation*. Assimilation ("to become similar") is the process of boundary reduction that occurs when two or more cultures meet (Yinger, 1981) by blending various cultural identities to form a new identity. The traditional metaphor associated with the process of assimilation has been the melting pot. However, in the United States, the melting pot became more a symbol of domination by White society, forcing those from different cultural backgrounds to relinquish their culture of origin in order to become members of the dominant culture. The new identity promulgated by the melting pot metaphor really became an expectation for all underrepresented groups to assume a White, Eurocentric identity, reject their own cultural backgrounds, and become totally absorbed by the majority culture. Assimilation implies a unidirectional movement and the superiority of a particular culture. This may have been easier when most newcomers to the United States were White and from Central Europe, but it became problematic when more and more immigrants were from nondominant racial backgrounds (Black, Asian, and Latino). Assimilation is most probable when there is a low identity with one's own nondominant culture and a high identity with the dominant culture (Smither, 1982).

Integration

The second form of boundary reduction that seeks to maintain a positive relationship with the dominant culture is called *integration* (Berry, 1980).

Unlike assimilation, integration allows one always to identify with the minority culture while becoming competent in the majority culture. However, LaFromboise, Coleman, and Gerton (1993) indicated that integration as a model of second-culture acquisition is like assimilation in that it implies the acquisition of the dominant culture, a unidirectional relationship toward the dominant culture, and a hierarchical relationship between the two cultures. These authors caution that in integration (and acculturative models in general) minorities are often relegated to accepting second-class citizenship within the majority group. In other words, the very term *acculturation* implies unidirectionality since a new identity is formed by moving toward the dominant culture and integrating its positive aspects without rejecting one's culture of origin.

Alternation

The *alternation* model of cultural adaptation implies a bidirectional and nonhierarchical relationship between two cultures. Unlike integration (which implies relinquishing some aspects of one's culture to replace them with another), alternation assumes that it is possible to know and understand two different cultures, and to maintain a positive relationship with both by altering one's behavior to fit the particular cultural context (LaFromboise, Coleman, & Gerton, 1993). The alternation model allows for biculturalism, the ability to maintain and develop competence in both cultures. Biculturalism differs from integrationism in that the latter results from the ability to foster a relationship between two cultures, whereas the former allows for relationships with two cultures that are not easily related or fused together. Biculturalism is facilitated by a multicultural society, one that values the diversity of cultural groups (Berry, 1980), and should not be confused with a plural society, which simply admits to the presence of different cultural groups.

Rejection

Unlike the previous forms of cultural adaptation, rejection does not seek a positive relationship with the other culture. Rejection by the dominant culture of the nondominant culture leads to separation. Rejection of the dominant culture by the nondominant culture results in withdrawal (Berry, 1980) caused by a high identification with one's minority culture and a low identification with the majority culture (Smither, 1982). In this scenario, one's cultural identity is maintained, but the possibility of biculturalism is eliminated.

Marginality

In the final category in the typology of cultural adaptation is the person who identifies with neither the dominant nor nondominant culture. In contrast to biculturalism, marginal people cannot relinquish the influence of the dominant culture but at the same time do not feel at home with their native culture (Weisberger, 1992). There is low identity with both the minority and majority cultures (Smither, 1982). Berry (1980) referred to this phenomenon as *deculturation* "in which groups [or individuals] are out of cultural and psychological contact with either their traditional culture or the larger society" (p. 15).

The foregoing typology helps to understand that individuals will respond to an intercultural encounter in a variety of ways. The form of adaptation and the amount of stress experienced depend on a multitude of variables interacting within the individual and between the native and host cultures.[1] The following section examines various models of interaction that serve to explain why an individual might assume one form of second-culture acquisition over another.

OBJECT RELATIONS THEORY AND CULTURAL ADAPTATION

The psychological perspective (understood as what goes on dynamically within the individual) on second-culture acquisition is derived mainly from object relations theory.

---

[1]For the purposes of this book, directed primarily for counselors in the United States, the phrase *native culture* is used interchangeably with *nondominant culture*, and *host culture* is used interchangeably with *dominant culture*. *Dominant* means the participants have a dominant share of political and economic power.

Infant Development and the Use of Self Objects

Winnicott (1966) understood cultural experience to be located in the *potential space* between the individual and the environment. At the beginning, the newborn baby is in a total narcissistic/symbiotic relationship with Mother. There is figuratively no "space" between infant and Mother, as the child is not able to distinguish self from object (Mother). As development occurs, the child begins to experience Mother as both nurturing and frustrating: The breast is both given and taken away—which leads to experiencing Mother as a "not me," an "object" different from the "subject" (the child), someone who comes and goes. Thus, there is created a space between child and Mother born out of the failure between need and gratification. In order to avoid the potentially overwhelming negative feelings of frustration and abandonment created by this space, the child learns to fill it with other objects (usually toys, but it can be anything) that are separate from—yet part of—self because they symbolize a connection between self and other (the mother or the outside world). In other words, the child learns to self-soothe (Applegate, 1990). Play is defined as the use of transitional objects in the area created by Mother's absence yet sustained by confidence and trust in her return. In this sense, the area of play both joins and separates the child with Mother. The area of play is the area of creative activity, the expression of the true self through the use of "self objects," defined as aspects of the human and nonhuman environment that are experienced as part of the self and nourish the self (Kohut, 1971, as quoted in Antokoletz, 1993).

Culture and Cultural Experience

Without defining the term *culture*, Winnicott (1966) located cultural experience in this space between self and environment. Culture provides the holding functions through objects, symbols, language, and so forth that help individuals (and the group to which they belong) mediate self and environment. These "self objects" provide a helpful and healthy transition between the needs of the self and the limitations of the environment. Culture, then, becomes part of the place where we live (Winnicott, 1971)—"the larger holding environment which is experienced as an elaboration of earliest feelings of familiarity and safety associated with primary caregivers" (Applegate, 1990, p. 88). From the object relations perspective, cultural groups are areas of familiarity, places of "play," offering comfort and security in an environment that would otherwise be frustrating and alienating. When the multiculturalists speak of culture as also including affiliative groups, the notion expands beyond ethnicity and race to include clubs, organizations, teams, and so forth where one feels loved, accepted, and "at home." The variations of the potential space are infinite and, in this sense, give credence to multiculturalism as a ubiquitous construct.

Cross-Cultural Experiences

Winnicott (1966) talked about the failure of the child's early environment as a loss in the potential space, the restriction of the development of the true self due to a lack of dependability of and confidence in the primary caregiver. The child is then forced to develop a false self or pseudo self in order to receive the necessary attention and nurturing. "Failure of dependability or loss of object means to the child a loss of the play area, and loss of meaningful symbol" (Winnicott, 1966, p. 371). The false self develops as a broker between the true self and the outside world.

Within the object relations perspective, cultural relocation precipitates a developmental crisis that reenacts the early childhood drama of negotiating the space between self and environment. The so-called holding environment has been changed, and the greater the discrepancy between the old and the new, the greater the psychological stress. Living in a new culture deprives the individual of the holding functions of the native culture (Antokoletz, 1993). The self objects of the potential space that were relied upon so heavily in the native culture to produce a sense of comfort and security with the surrounding environment are no longer available. This loss of object constancy launches the sojourner into a search for new transitional objects to mediate self and environment, to fill the potential space—the location of the cultural experience. If such objects are readily available, the adaptation process could be relatively smooth, with a minimal amount of stress. However, if the new environment does not offer viable self objects, stress can increase to the point of becoming culture shock—in which psychological needs are so deprived as to become manifested in clinical symptoms. One is forced to act in unfamiliar ways in a constant attempt to satisfy his or her needs, resulting in an exaggerated false self and an impoverished true self. Cross-cultural counseling within this perspective would have to create an environment of trust in which the client feels safe enough to once again "play" in the potential space incorporating new self objects. The first of these objects may very well be the counselor and, eventually, a network of objects provide the nurturing and validating functions of the native culture (Antokoletz, 1993).

From this object relations perspective, the process of second-culture acquisition as it relates to counseling can be divided into three phases (Antokoletz, 1993; Garza-Guerrero, 1974). The first is mourning the loss of the native culture (i.e., grieving the loss of love objects). During this phase, one seeks relief in past relationships (objects) that provided comfort and soothing. In this phase, there is a tendency to idealize the native culture, to accentuate the affective link as a defense mechanism against loss and melancholy. There needs also to be a working through of anger and helplessness associated with the host culture, which may be experienced as rejecting and prejudicial. In the second phase, there can be a gradual acceptance of the new culture that involves intrapsychic reorganization— the reexamination and reshaping of past object relations and introducing new ones available from the host culture. During this time, the immigrant is reworking the holding environment. The final phase is marked by a synthesis or integration or alternation of self objects from both the native and host culture, which results in a remodeled ego identity or bicultural identity.

Thus, even in a traditional analytical perspective, the goal is a healthy integration or alternation of the two cultures. If one is an integrationist, the development of second-culture acquisition will result in having one set of self objects that facilitate a feeling of being at home in both cultures. Development around the alternation model of second-culture acquisition will result in having two sets of objects, allowing one to move from one culture to another with ease and a sense of familiarity.

This section has explored an exclusively intrapsychic explanation of cultural adaptation. Though valuable for understanding one dimension of the process, the object relations perspective needs to be complemented with theories that consider other psychological variables, along with cognitive and social variables, affecting cultural adaptation.

PSYCHOLOGICAL ROLE THEORY

Psychological role theory takes into consideration not only the character structure but also the role structure of an individual in explaining the varieties of cultural adaptation. A person's role is defined as a "pattern or type of social behavior which seems situationally appropriate to him in terms of the demands and expectations of his groups" (Sargent, 1951, as quoted in Smither, 1982). However, individuals from the same group take on different roles—a difference explained by the character structure that determines the comfort and success level an individual will enjoy by assuming a given role. Therefore, acculturation (understood as the process of becoming identified to some degree with the dominant culture) would mean assuming a role (or roles) valued by the dominant culture (Smither, 1982). The degree of difficulty in assuming such a role is proportionate to the degree of difference between an individual's role as played in the non-dominant culture and as played in the dominant culture, along with variables of character structure. Variables in character structure affecting cultural adaptation have been identified from evolutionary and anthropological theory as intellect, adjustment, prudence, assertiveness, likability, sociability, and ego control (Hogan & Johnson, 1979). Though this is an incomplete taxonomy of personality, low levels of these qualities would make cultural adjustment more difficult (Smither, 1982); combined with a large degree of role discrepancy, such inadequacies would make adjustment stressful and perhaps "shocking." Constants such as age, race, and level of education must also be factored into the equation.

Thus, a counselor needs to keep in mind these dimensions of role and character structure involved in the adaptation process, as they can account for both intergroup and intragroup differences. Theoretically, a middle-aged, fairly educated individual from a large city in Southeast Asia will have a more difficult process of second-culture acquisition in the United States than will a youngster from Ireland. However, this same Asian would have an easier time than an elderly poor farmer from the same country. Furthermore, in comparison to a peer with the same demographic background, the process of second-culture acquisition can vary because of differences in character structure. Whether character structure variables override demographic variables is a subject of controversy and requires future research.

COGNITIVE THEORY AND CULTURAL ADAPTATION

More cognitive models of cultural adaptation rely on principles of learning theory and thus view the experience as an opportunity for growth and learning rather than a problem (Taylor, 1994). Cultural adaptability is viewed as "the individual's capacity to suspend or modify some of the old cultural ways, [and] to *learn* and accommodate some of the new cultural ways..." (Kim, 1991, p. 268, as quoted in Taylor, 1994). The word *accommodate* associated with learning harkens back to Piaget's (1966) theory of cognitive development. When new information no longer fits the cognitive structures ("schema"), the child *accommodates* to the new stimuli by changing the schema. In accommodation, the organism changes to fit the environment (Woldemikael, 1987). When this process was applied to cultural adaptation, Taylor (1994) talked about it as transformative learning, involving a change of perspective (perspective is understood as a collection of schema), "the process of making a new or revised interpretation of the meaning of an experience, which guides subsequent understanding, appreciation, and action" (Mezirow, 1991, as quoted in Taylor, 1994, p. 395). When applied to issues of second-culture acquisition, "transformative learning attempts to explain how our expectations, framed within cultural assumptions and presuppositions, directly influence the meaning we derive from our experiences" (Taylor, 1994, p. 395). Thus, our cultural background is responsible for the formation of meaning perspectives that act as perceptual filters that organize the meaning of our experiences (Taylor, 1994). As new experiences occur, they are interpreted and given meaning through these perceptual filters. They are "assimilated"—Piaget's (1952) word for how children incorporate and interpret new information in terms of their present cognitive structures.

However, there are times when an individual undergoes radical new experiences (often the case when living in a different culture) that cannot be assimilated. In such cases, the individual has the option of rejecting the experience or changing the meaning perspective to accommodate the new experience (Taylor, 1994), which involves the reappraisal of previous assumptions. Either option attempts to reduce the stress caused by experiences having an alienating and disorienting effect upon the organism. If the approach is to accommodate the new experience, the individual moves toward a more flexible, permeable, inclusive, and integrated worldview (Kim, 1988; Mezirow, 1991; Taylor, 1994). For example, a White Euro-American would be challenged to relinquish cultural assumptions of individualism to understand (accommodate) the group-over-individual approach to life of Native American and African American cultures. This is not the simple acquisition of intellectual knowledge about another culture. Transformative learning involves critical self-reflection and reappraisal of one's way of seeing things (perceptual filters) as well as sustaining the challenge caused by such a process. If the capacity for transformative learning (perspective transformation) is minimal for whatever reason, withdrawal from or rejection of the culturally different is the most likely scenario. Accommodation would be a defining cognitive characteristic of those who achieve second-culture acquisition, through either integration or alternation. Accommodation allows for bidirectionality and multidirectionality in the process of cultural adaptation; its absence would favor a unidirectional approach.

Finally, transformative learning theory posits culture as a template for organizing cognitive processes. In this sense, it is a helpful construct for understanding the cognitive dimension of the second-culture acquisition process. Furthermore, transformative learning theory provides the interface between multiculturalism and postmodernism.

Meaning-Making Transformation and Postmodernism

Human beings are unique in that they are meaning-making animals. Humans not only experience, but attempt to make meaning out of their experiences. Previously, successful cross-cultural encounters were seen as requiring a change in meaning-making perspectives to accommodate radically new experiences. Different cultures have different meanings for the same experience. For example, our scientific culture tells us that thunder is the result of variables in atmospheric pressure—in contrast to a religious culture that understands thunder as the expression of angry gods. Both cultures are trying to make meaning out of experience, and these meanings become codified in language, or story, or narrative. Consequently, a change in meaning-making perspective would result in a different story or narrative about the experience. Since stories are relative (across cultures), rather than inhabiting a universe of truths, we inhabit a universe of stories (Parry, 1991). The reification and imposition of one story over another is simply the result of historical and psychological conditions (Pare, 1996) and not the "truth" or "scientific nature" of such stories. In the postmodern movement, philosophy of science is replaced by the history and sociology of knowledge. For example, Freud's "story" about human development (i.e., the psychosexual stages) for the longest time was embraced as truth because of both its provocative nature (sexuality as the all-determining factor in human development) and the historical conditions (the repression of sexuality) in which the "story" was told. Rather than talking about one interpretation (story) as being truer than another, postmodernism encourages us to look at the historical and cultural processes that privilege some stories while suppressing others (McNamee & Gergen, 1992; Pare, 1996). In cross-cultural encounters, stories about experience come into conflict, and cultural domination can be seen as having the power and influence to impose one story over another.

Implications for Counseling

The culturally sensitive counselor can draw from both the transformative learning approach to cultural adaptation and narrative counseling. If all that exists are stories about experience, the first step would be to access clients' stories, which equate to their version of reality, their way of making meaning out of experience, a result of their cultural background. From a perspective of second-culture acquisition, problems arise for the sojourner when the power of the dominant culture does not allow for alternate discourses in organizing reality, when the private, local, idiosyncratic conversations of the sojourner are suppressed and marginalized by broader cultural discourses. The goal of counseling then becomes the facilitation of a more workable fit between the two cultures. The aim is a bicultural effectiveness that allows an individual to operate competently in settings organized by the dominant culture, while preserving desired elements of his or her own cultural heritage. Berry and Kim (1988) studied levels of stress according to modes of cultural adaptation and found (1) the most stress among the marginalized and separated, (2) an intermediate amount of stress among the assimilated, and (3) the least amount of stress among those who achieved a level of biculturalism.

The role of the counselor within this cognitive framework becomes the facilitation of the cultural narrative, alternate narratives, and a less disturbed posture in observing the way others make meaning out of experience. This can range from a simple awareness of and respect for other cultural narratives to the actual integration (not substitution) of alternate narratives as a way of enriching one's meaning-making practices. This adaptation process begins at a definite point in time—when the individual acknowledges either emotionally, cognitively, or behaviorally the existence of obstacles and a decision to work on a strategy for overcoming such obstacles (Anderson, 1994). In contrast, it is difficult to determine when the adaptation process ends, as some believe the achievement of a bicultural identity can be a lifelong process (Anderson, 1994). Most likely, the endpoint has to do with feelings of belonging, of fitting in, and the reduction or complete absence of stress related to a new environment.

Before moving on, a more careful examination of the phenomenon of stress related to cultural adaptation is necessary, since cultural adaptation is the most likely cause of stress-related symptoms among those from nondominant cultures who appear for counseling services.

ACCULTURATIVE STRESS AND MENTAL HEALTH

Several allusions have been made to the fact that, when two different cultures come into contact, a complex cognitive process with emotional consequences is put into motion. There have also been references to the many variables regulating the amount of stress, and the term *cultural adaptation* has been used in a normalizing fashion to refer to the transitional experience one undergoes in a new environment. This experience can be stressful yet exhilarating, demanding yet joyful. However, the question arises as to when the adaptation process, necessary and normal, becomes a clinical issue. Counselors need to prepare themselves for those clients whose second-culture acquisition processes have become too demanding and led them to seek therapeutic services. As our population becomes increasingly diverse, one should not underestimate the psychological effects of racism practiced by the dominant culture—especially upon non-Whites arriving in the United States.

Accultural Stress Versus Culture Shock

In recent years, the term *acculturative stress* has been used increasingly as a generic reference to emotional difficulties associated with transition to a new environment (Williams & Berry, 1991). Discussion of different stress levels associated with acculturation has replaced, at least in psychological circles, the much referred to syndrome of "culture shock" (Furnham & Bochner, 1986). As mentioned earlier, variables within the individual, as well as contrasts between the dominant and nondominant cultures, account for different levels of stress. However, some writers (Anderson, 1994; Taylor, 1994) reserve the term *culture shock* for severe levels of accultural stress that result in an extreme lack of capacity to function in the new environment. In general, stress is the result of a mismatch between the demands of the environment and an individual's perceived capacity to cope with such demands (Lazarus & Folkman, 1984).

Models of Acculturative Stress

Various models of acculturative stress have developed over the years as a result of work with specific groups: refugees (Williams & Berry, 1991); Black Americans (Anderson, 1991); and Hispanics (Smart & Smart, 1995). Williams and Berry (1991) list five factors that regulate the relationship between acculturation and stress:

1. The mode of acculturation (integration, assimilation, separation, and marginalization)

2. The phase of acculturation (contact, conflict, crisis, adaptation)

3. The nature of the larger society (multicultural vs. assimilationist; prejudiced and discriminatory)

4. Characteristics of the adapting group (age, status, and social support)

5. Characteristics of the acculturating individual (appraisal, coping attitudes, contact)

The second-culture acquisition modes of separation and marginalization produce more stress, as do the phases of conflict and crisis. So too, a less plural host society rift with prejudice and discrimination would be more stressful than would a multicultural society. Regarding status, lower socioeconomic and less educated groups experience more stress than those with more resources. Social support is the most comprehensive variable in moderating stress, and those groups with developed ethnic and cultural networks will suffer less stress. Finally, alongside social variables, there exists a host of intrapersonal variables that regulate the amount of stress. Individual characteristics such as good coping mechanisms and positive contacts in the larger society will contribute to stress reduction. Thus, counselors working with immigrants need to make themselves aware of the clients' mode and phase of acculturation, their experience of discrimination by the larger society, their status within their own group and in relationship to the host society, their social support system, and operative intrapsychic variables related to stress.

Anderson (1991), in dealing with Black Americans, developed a heuristic model of acculturative stress from Lazarus (1984) and Kaplan (1983). After identifying three source levels of stress, Anderson (1991) focused on more specific cultural factors among Black Americans—such as patterns of living, cultural values, and cultural identity—which, depending on their degree of discrepancy from the dominant culture, can be a source of more or less stress (Smart & Smart, 1995). Anderson (1991) refered to empirical data suggesting that Black Americans suffer more stress at each of these levels than Whites. One could extrapolate and say the same would be true for other nondominant groups—especially those that are poor and of a different racial background than the dominant culture. Like that of Williams and Berry (1991), the Anderson model considers mediating factors such as cognitive appraisal, self-esteem, and social support. These are interrelated in that cognitive appraisal has to do with issues of self-efficacy in facing and overcoming the challenges created by stressful conditions. In turn, those with good self-esteem are more able to access and become part of social support systems. Once again, a combination of internal and external variables will account for psychological and physical distress resulting from the acculturative process.

Smart and Smart (1995) list the many consequences in daily living that are the result of acculturative stress. Empirical support exists for the following. Acculturative stress affects physical health and can result in numerous somatic complaints (Smith, 1985). High levels of stress also affect decision making (Hinkle, 1974). Feeling that their options are limited, depressed individuals may consider suicide as the only way out (Smart & Smart, 1995). Acculturative stress also affects occupational functioning, as many immigrants are ill-prepared for the current technological demands in the workplace.

Regarding counseling, second-culture acquisition stress can contribute to "strained and ineffective counselor-client relations" (Smart & Smart, 1995, p. 32). A combination of cultural insensitivity on the part of the counselor combined with the client's discomfort in relating cross-culturally will make establishment of the working alliance quite challenging. The effects of these possible clinical manifestations of stress should not be ignored or minimized by the counselor working with clients from nondominant cultures.

In conclusion, not all processes of cultural adaptation will be clinically stressful. In fact, some may be stressful in a healthy sense—as with physical exercise: challenging but rewarding. However, until we live in a truly multicultural society, one that permits fair access to power for all cultural groups formed by race, ethnicity, gender, and sexual orientation, the strong possibility exists that the stress produced from being a member of a nondominant culture will be overwhelming.

MEASURES OF ACCULTURATION

Over the years, numerous measures of acculturation have been developed for various groups. Some of these are designed for general use with racial/ethnic groups, while others are for specific groups within a particular racial category. Examples of the former are the African American Acculturation Scale (Landrine & Klonoff, 1994, 1995), the Suinn-Lew Asian Self-Identity Acculturation Scale (Suinn, Rickard-Figueroa, Lew, & Vigil, 1987), and the Acculturation Scale for Hispanics (Marin, Sabogal, Marin, & Otero-Sabogal, 1987). Examples of intragroup measures of acculturation include the Acculturation Rating Scale for Mexican Americans (Cuellar, Arnold, & Maldonado, 1995; Cuellar, Harris, & Jasso, 1980); the Greek American Acculturation Scale (Harris & Verven, 1996); the Taiwan Aboriginal Acculturation Scale (Cheng & Hsu, 1995); the Hawaiian Acculturation Scale (Rezentes, 1993); and the Acculturation Scale for Southeast Asians (Anderson, Moeschberger, Chen, & Kunn, 1993). Measures of acculturation tend to adopt a standard Likert-scale format of behaviors indicative of the subject's native culture and the dominant culture. These behaviors may include food preferences, celebration of holidays, socialization experiences, relationship with family, contacts with the native country, and dominant language facility. The goal of these measures is to quantify placement along a continuum bounded by two polarities, the native culture and the dominant culture, and thus assess the level of acculturation. Although it is beyond the scope of this book to examine all the currently existing measures of acculturation, the following section examines three of the more well known and utilized.

Acculturation Rating Scale for Mexican Americans (ARSMA)

The ARSMA is one of the more researched measures of acculturation and was originally developed in 1980 by Cuellar, Harris, and Jasso. Recently, the ARSMA was revised (ARSMA II, Cuellar, Arnold, & Maldonado, 1995). The original ARSMA had 20 Likert-type items and revealed a coefficient alpha of .88 and test-retest reliability of .72. Content, construct, discriminant, and convergent validity have been supported for the ARSMA (Ponterotto & Casas, 1991). Confirmatory factor analyses have also been performed on the ARSMA that indicate that acculturation involves historical familial identification, contacts with Mexico, ease with reading and writing Spanish, socializing with friends, and selecting foods (Orozco, Thompson, Kapes, & Montgomery, 1993). The revised version of the ARSMA requires further research. However, incipient data suggest good internal reliabilities and a high correlation with the original scale (Cuellar, Arnold, & Maldonado, 1995).

Suinn-Lew Asian Self-Identity Acculturation Scale (SL-ASIA)

The SL-ASIA was first developed as a measure of acculturation in 1987 and has been widely used in the last 10 years in spite of the limited research that has been done on the scale. The developers of the SL-ASIA (Suinn, Rickard-Figueroa, Lew, & Vigil, 1987) reported Cronbach's alpha for internal consistency of .88 compared to .91 in a later study by Suinn, Ahuna, and Khoo (1992). Suinn, Ahuna, and Khoo (1992), using a much larger sample of 324 Asian American students, demonstrated concurrent validity with significant correlations between SL-ASIA scores and demographic information such as number of years living and attending school in the United States, age upon arriving in the United States, and years living in a non-Asian neighborhood.

Kodama and Canetto (1995) used the SL-ASIA with Japanese temporary residents and found a significant correlation between the SL-ASIA scores and self-ratings of acculturation. However, internal consistency was lower than in studies where the SL-ASIA was used with Asian Americans. In contrast to Suinn, Ahuna, and Khoo (1992), Kodama and Canetto (1995) found no significant correlation between SL-ASIA scores and demographic data assumed to reflect levels of acculturation. Given the rapidly increasing numbers of Asian Americans in this country and the relatively few instruments available for measuring their level of acculturation, there is a definite need for more research on the SL-ASIA, involving different groups of Asian Americans to support intergroup reliability and validity.

African American Acculturation Scale (AAAS)

The AAAS is a recently developed instrument (Landrine & Klonoff, 1994) for which a short form (AAAS-33)—consisting of 33 items as compared to 74 in the long form—has also been created (Landrine & Klonoff, 1995). Designed to measure Blacks' identification with African culture, the AAAS consists of eight subscales reflecting eight dimensions of African American culture and was first tested on a cross-racial sample of 183 subjects. Analyses on the original sample (Landrine & Klonoff, 1994) indicated high internal consistency reliability ranging from .71 to .90 for the different subscales and split-half reliability of .93 for the scale as a whole. Criterion-related validity was supported by a highly signifi-cant difference between scores for African Americans and non-African Americans.

In a cross-validation study of the AAAS, Landrine and Klonoff (1995) found internal consistency to remain relatively stable. Further results in-dicated that younger African Americans living in predominantly White neighborhoods obtained scores on the AAAS similar to the original sam-ple of older African Americans living in predominantly Black neighbor-hoods. Combined with the data from the original sample of 123 African Americans, factor analyses were performed rendering the shorter version of the AAAS, consisting of 33 items, assessing 10 factors of African Amer-ican culture. These 33 items indicated an internal consistency ranging from .42 (Family Practices) to .89 (Preference for Things African Ameri-can) for the 10 subscales and split-half reliability of .78 (Landrine & Klonoff, 1995). Furthermore, scores on the AAAS-33 correlated highly ($r = .94$) with the original and longer AAAS. Data indicated that the African American subjects living in Black neighborhoods scored signifi-cantly higher on eight of the 10 subscales than those living elsewhere. This difference supports the concurrent validity of the AAAS-33 and, combined with the data reported above, appears to make the AAAS-33 a viable alternative to the long form.

Alongside the numerous instruments measuring Black identity (atti-tudes of African Americans toward their Blackness), the AAAS and the AAAS-33 are the only instruments attempting to measure levels of accul-turation for African Americans. While the authors themselves recognize the need for further work on the scales, the incipient radiability and validity data are encouraging. Therefore, the AAAS and the AAAS-33 promise to be valuable instruments for those researchers and clinicians wishing to quantify African Americans' identification with African culture versus identification with the mainstream, White culture of the United States.

Use of Acculturation Measures

As a result of this discussion, the reader has perhaps become aware of the problems associated with measures of acculturation. They are typically the result of a unidirectional conceptualization of second-culture acquisition. Most acculturation measures attempt to quantify movement from the culture of origin toward the dominant culture. In view of a more recent understanding of second-culture acquisition as bidirectional and multidirectional, these measures of acculturation should be used circumspectly. In addition to the problem of unilinear measurement, Marin (1992) has criticized acculturation measures for Hispanics as lacking in psychometric properties; overrelying on language use and proficiency; and failing to consider important variables such as cognitive style, personality, and attitudes.

The ARSMA-II (Cuellar, Arnold, & Maldonado, 1995) has attempted to move beyond the unidirectional measures of acculturation by having a scale divided into the Anglo Orientation Subscale (AOS) and Mexican Orientation Subscale (MOS). The two subscales can be used independently, as measures of biculturalism, and dependently by subtracting one score from the other to yield a single linear acculturation score (Atkinson, Morton, & Sue, 1998). Previously to the ARSMA-II, Szapocznik, Kurtines, and Fernandez (1980) developed the Bicultural Involvement Questionnaire, again yielding two separate and independent scores for a client's involvement in Hispanic and European-American cultures (Atkinson, Morton, & Sue, 1998).

While measures of acculturation may serve the purpose of initial assessment, they tend to oversimplify the process of second-culture acquisition. However, recent developments in this field prove promising as the process of cultural adaptation is increasingly understood as more multidimensional and multidirectional than previously thought.

SUMMARY

The construct of second-culture acquisition is a necessary and valuable tool for counselors working with clients from diverse cultural backgrounds. Knowledge of clients' native culture and their current relationship with the host culture can be the focal points of the counseling relationship. Problems in the second-culture acquisition experience must be assessed along the lines of character structure, demographic variables, and degree of discrepancy between the two cultures. Counselors must conceptualize the form of cultural adaptation that a particular client is assuming and the degree it is helpful or harmful to psychological well-being. If it is harmful, the role of the counselor becomes the facilitation of a more workable fit between the two cultures. The second part of this book examines particular ways a counselor might accomplish this task.

REFERENCES

Anderson, L. (1991). Acculturative stress: A theory of relevance to Black Americans. *Clinical Psychology Review 11*, 685–702.

Anderson, L.E. (1994). A new look at an old construct: Cross cultural adaptation. *International Journal of Intercultural Relations, 18*, 293–328.

Anderson, J., Moeschberger, M., Chen, M.S., & Kunn, P. (1993). An acculturation scale for Southeast Asians. *Social Psychiatry and Psychiatric Epidemiology, 28*, 134–141.

Antokoletz, J.C. (1993). A psychoanalytic view of cross-cultural passages. *The American Journal of Psychoanalysis, 53*, 35–54.

Applegate, J.S. (1990). Theory, culture, and behavior: Object relations in context. *Child and Adolescent Social Work, 7*, 85–100.

Atkinson, D.R., Morton, G., & Sue, D.W. (1998). *Counseling American minorities* (5th ed.). Boston: McGraw-Hill.

Berry, J.W. (1980). Acculturation as variety of adaptation. In A.M. Padilla (Ed.), *Acculturation: Theory, models and some new findings*. Washington, DC: AAAS.

Berry, J.W., & Kim, U. (1988). Acculturation and mental health. In P. Dasen, J.W. Berry, & N. Sartorius (Eds.), *Health and cross-cultural psychology* (pp. 207–236). Newbury Park, CA: Sage.

Cheng, A.T., & Hsu, M. (1995). Development of a new scale for measuring acculturation: The Taiwan Aboriginal Acculturation Scale (TAAS). *Psychological Medicine, 25*, 1281–1287.

Cuellar, I., Arnold, B., & Maldonado, R. (1995). Acculturation Rating Scale for Mexican Americans II: A revision of the original ARSMA Scale. *Hispanic Journal of Behavioral Sciences, 17,* 275–304.

Cuellar, I., Harris, L.C., & Jasso, R. (1980). An acculturation scale for Mexican American normal and clinical populations. *Hispanic Journal of Behavioral Sciences, 2,* 199–217.

Furnham, A., & Bochner, S. (1986). *Culture shock: Psychological reactions to unfamiliar environments.* London: Methuen.

Garza-Guerrero, A.C. (1974). Culture shock: Its mourning and the vicissitudes of identity. *Journal of the American Psychoanalytic Association, 22,* 408–429.

Harris, A.C., & Verven, R. (1996). The Greek–American Acculturation Scale: Development and validity. *Psychological Reports, 78,* 599–610.

Hinkle, L.E. (1974). The effect of exposure to cultural change, social change, and changes in interpersonal relationships on health. In B.S. Dohrenwend & B.P. Dohrenwend (Eds.), *Stressful life events: The nature and effects* (pp. 9–44). New York: Wiley.

Hogan, R., & Johnson, J. (1979). *The Hopkins Personality Inventory: A psychoanalytic view of the structure of personality.* Unpublished manuscript, Johns Hopkins University, 1979.

Kaplan, H. (Ed.). (1983). *Psychosocial stress.* New York: Academic Press.

Kim, Y.Y. (1988). *Communication and cross cultural adaptation: An integrative theory.* Philadelphia: Multilingual Matters.

Kodama, K., & Canetto, S.S. (1995). Reliability and validity of the Suinn–Lew Asian Self-Identity Acculturation Scale with Japanese temporary residents. *Psychologia, 38,* 17–21.

LaFromboise, T., Coleman, H.L., & Gerton, J. (1993). Psychological impact of biculturalism: Evidence and theory. *Psychological Bulletin, 114,* 395–412.

Landrine, H., & Klonoff, E.A. (1994). The African American Acculturation Scale: Development, reliability, and validity. *Journal of Black Psychology, 20,* 104–127.

Landrine, H., & Klonoff, E.A. (1995). The African American Acculturation Scale II: Cross validation and short form. *Journal of Black Psychology, 21,* 124–152.

Lazarus, R.S. (1984). Puzzles in the study of daily hassles. *Journal of Behavioral Medicine, 7,* 375–384.

Lazarus, R.S., & Folkman, S. (1984). *Stress, appraisal, and coping.* New York: Springer.

Marin, G. (1992). Issues in the measurement of acculturation among Hispanics. In K.F. Geisinger (Ed.), *Psychological testing of Hispanics* (pp. 235–251). Washington, DC: American Psychological Association.

Marin, G., Sabogal, F., Marin, B.V., & Otero-Sabogal, R. (1987). Development of a short acculturation scale of Hispanics. *Hispanic Journal of Behavioral Sciences, 9,* 183–205.

McNamee, S., & Gergen, K.J. (Eds.). (1992). *Therapy as social construction.* Newbury Park, CA: Sage.

Mezirow, J. (1991) *Transformative dimensions of adult learning*. San Francisco: Jossey-Bass.

Orozco, S., Thompson, B., Kapes, J., & Montgomery, G.T. (1993). Measuring the acculturation of Mexican Americans. *Measurement and Evaluation in Counseling and Development, 25,* 149–155.

Pare, D.A. (1996). Culture and meaning: Expanding the metaphorical repertoire of family therapy. *Family Process, 35,* 21–42.

Parry, A. (1991). A universe of stories. *Family Process, 30,* 37–54.

Piaget, J. (1952). *The origins of intelligence in children.* New York: International Universities Press.

Piaget, J. (1966). *Psychology of intelligence.* Totowa, NJ: Littlefield, Adams, & Co.

Ponterotto, J.G., & Casas, J.M. (1991). *Handbook of racial/ethnic minority counseling research.* Springfield, IL: Charles C. Thomas.

Rezentes, W.C. (1993). Na Mea Hawai'i: A Hawaiian acculturation scale. *Psychological Reports, 73,* 383–393.

Smart, J.F., & Smart, D.W. (1995). Acculturative stress: The experience of the Hispanic immigrant. *The Counseling Psychologist, 23,* 25–42.

Smith, E.M. (1985). Ethnic minorities: Life stress, social support, and mental health issues. *The Counseling Psychologist, 13,* 537–579.

Smither, R. (1982). Human migration and the acculturation of minorities. *Human Relations, 35,* 57–68.

Suinn, R.M., Ahuna, C., & Khoo, G. (1992). The Suinn-Lew Asian Self-Identity Acculturation Scale: Concurrent and factorial validation. *Educational and Psychological Measurement, 52,* 1041–1046.

Suinn, R.M., Rickard-Figueroa, K., Lew, S., & Vigil, P. (1987). The Suinn-Lew Asian Self-Identity Scale: An initial report. *Educational and Psychological Measurement, 47,* 400–407.

Szapocznik, J., Kurtines, W., & Fernandez, T. (1980). Bicultural involvement and adjustment in Hispanic-American youths. *International Journal of Intercultural Relations, 4,* 401–407.

Taylor, E.W. (1994). A learning model for becoming interculturally competent. *International Journal of Intercultural Relations, 18,* 389–408.

Weisberger, A. (1992). Marginality and its directions. *Sociological Forum, 7,* 425–446.

Williams, C.L., & Berry, J.W. (1991). Primary prevention of acculturative stress among refugees. *American Psychologist, 46,* 632–641.

Winnicott, D.W. (1966). The location of cultural experience. *International Journal of Psychoanalysis, 48,* 368–372.

Winnicott, D.W. (1971). *Playing and reality.* London: Tavistock.

Woldemikael, T.M. (1987). Assertion versus accommodation. *American Behavioral Scientist, 30,* 411–428.

Yinger, J.M. (1981). Toward a theory of assimilation and dissimilation. *Ethnic and Racial Studies, 4,* 249–264.

CHAPTER 3

—*ᘓᐭᐭᘏ*—

CULTURAL IDENTITY DEVELOPMENT

Hoare (1991), referring to Erikson's ideas, defines identity as the partly conscious, largely unconscious sense of who one is, both as person and as contributor to society. "Both unconscious and conscious, identity is personal coherence of self-sameness through evolving time, social change and altered role requirements" (Hoare, 1991, p. 47). Cultural identity development theory posits that members of a particular cultural group go through different stages or statuses marked by different attitudes toward their own and other cultural groups. Attitudes and behaviors are the result of complex cognitive and emotional processes around the relationship people have to their own cultural group. This relationship in turn determines the relationship they have with cultural groups different than their own. The previous chapter examined the forms, challenges, stressors, and rewards of second-culture acquisition. The present chapter examines more closely the developmental process perhaps responsible for the form, or lack thereof, of second-culture acquisition.

Since the earliest models of cultural identity development were related to race and particularly Black identity development, this chapter will begin with the psychology of Nigrescence and trace the development of other cultural identity theories. According to Helms, racial identity "refers to a sense of group or collective identity based on one's *perception* that he or she shares a common racial heritage with a particular racial group" (Helms, 1990a, p. 3). Racial identity has to do with belief systems regarding racial group membership and the quality and/or manner of such membership. On the other hand, the simple term *race* refers to more biologically driven characteristics devoid of psychological attitudes and belief systems.

THE PSYCHOLOGY OF NIGRESCENCE

Helms (1990b) articulated at least 11 Nigrescence models of racial identity that developed between 1971 and 1984. Though developed in different regions of the country, the 11 models are strikingly similar in that all outlined the healthy development of Blacks as moving away from an overidentification with Whites and White culture to a psychological and socially rewarding acceptance and appreciation of Blackness.

The Cross Model

Cross (1971) was one of the first to publish a stage model regarding Black identity development, which he called "Nigrescence," becoming Black "in terms of one's manner of thinking about and evaluating oneself and one's reference groups rather than in terms of skin color per se" (Helms, 1990a, p. 17). Besides being one of the first, the Cross model imposed itself over the years due to its facility in measurement. The Cross model posits five stages of Black identity development that he termed preencounter, encounter, immersion-emersion, internalization, and internalization-commitment.

Preencounter. A Black person at this stage basically has a Eurocentric view of the world, a tendency to deny one's Blackness, and therefore a desire to assimilate the ways of the majority race. "White is right" is the fundamental attitude at this stage. The belief system involves moving forward in life by disassociating oneself with anything or anyone Black and adopting the ways of White society. The preencounter attitude manifests itself outwardly through such things as dress, hairstyle, and choice of friends—as all of these are orchestrated to "look White."

Encounter. At some point, preencounter individuals undergo an experience (an "encounter") either positive or negative that makes them begin to question the fundamental attitude of the preencounter stage. This encounter may be with another person, a book, a movie, or any experience that allows the individual to reflect upon his or her own identity of being Black. It is a stage marked by confusion and soul-searching, as the person is still uncomfortable with his or her Blackness but at the same time uncomfortable with trying to be White. The individual feels at home neither in White nor Black society, and there is a tendency to want to be seen as just a "human being" devoid of any racial identity (Ford, Harris, & Schuerger, 1993).

Immersion-Emersion. The first phase of this stage (immersion) is marked by a radical rejection of Whiteness and the first attempts to forge a new identity as a Black person. The "White is right" attitude of the preencounter stage is replaced by "White is evil" and "Black is beautiful" and even superior. Thus, the absence of melanin becomes a sign of inferiority (in direct contrast to White supremacists). It is a stage marked by dichotomous thinking in which everything like me is good and everything not like me is not good. This attitude is manifested by, among other things, wearing only African dress, having an African hairstyle, seeing Black friends, and perhaps adopting African names. The second phase (emersion) represents an emergence from the radical immersion into one's own group, a so-called leveling off, and a less rigid stance before those who are not Black. Still maintaining a Black worldview, this person is more proactive and less reactive (Helms, 1990a).

Internalization. Here, the person has internalized a true sense of Black identity that is positive, self-loving, flexible, and open to new experiences. It is an identity forged not so much by the hatred and rejection of others, but by a true appreciation and love of Blackness. This person is even open to incorporating the advantageous and supportive aspects of White society.

Feeling secure in one's own identity, there is more of an openness to those who are different.

Internalization-Commitment. This stage is marked by the same sense of identity as the previous stage, with the added dimension of social and political commitment. Having achieved a firm sense of identity, this Black person now becomes politically active against causes of oppression—not only for Black people but for other minority groups as well.

Though the Cross model has been criticized, especially for its simplicity (Parham, 1989), it has sustained itself over the last 20 years. Most other models of racial identity and cultural identity have been spin-offs of the original Cross model. Nevertheless, Cross himself has seen the need for revision and recently updated the model to consider the results and effects of research over the last 20 years (Cross, 1995).

The Revised Cross Model

Though the five stages remain the same in the revised model, Cross (1995) admits to the need for redefining the dynamics of certain stages, especially those of preencounter and internalization.

Preencounter. It was originally hypothesized that those at the preencounter stage would suffer from problems of low self-esteem, self-hate, high anxiety, and poor ego-integration. In short, the mental health of those at the preencounter stage would be compromised. It was further hypothesized that as one moved through the stages of Nigrescence, higher levels of mental health would accompany the journey. According to Cross (1995), research findings have failed to support the psychological dynamics positing that the majority of people at the preencounter stage are self-hating. As a result, Cross prefers to talk less in terms of psychological and more in terms of socialization dynamics. For example, those at the preencounter stage are said to give low precedence to racial issues. The preencounter person embraces an "outlook on life which simply downplays the significance of race" (Cross, 1995, p. 97). If anything, race is a problem, a stigma, something that gets in the way and therefore should not be given much importance. Cross concludes: "The key factors that separate Pre-Encounter Blacks from those who are Afrocentric are not mental illness, but value orientation, historical perspective, and worldview" (Cross, 1995, p. 104).

Further empirical evidence has led to the postulation of two forms of preencounter: active and passive (Cross, Parham, & Helms, 1991). The active phase is similar to Cross's description of a preencounter Black in the original model. However, the passive phase is something new that places less emphasis on direct actions to appear White and more on simple acceptance of White as the primary reference group. These Blacks have a very internal attributional style and refrain from the suggestion that race or racial indoctrination has anything to do with how they live their lives (Helms, 1990b).

Internalization. The same revision of the preencounter stage was also necessary for the internalization stage. Rather than personality change or a change in mental health status, the internalization stage is marked primarily by a change in the degree of priority given to race and racial issues, along with a change in the person's primary reference group. The movement from immersion-emersion to the internalization stage is "from anxious, insecure, rigid, pseudo-Blackness based on the hatred of Whites, to proactive Black pride, self-love, and a deep sense of connection to, and acceptance by, the Black community" (Cross, 1995, p. 113). However, ideological perspectives can be divergent at the advanced stages of Nigrescence, whereas in the earlier model they were thought to be quite unified. Cross (1995) attributes this to continued growth and influence of the Afrocentric and Black Nationalist Movements whose adherents evidence advanced stages of Nigrescence and are not at the immersion-emersion stage. On the other hand, Blacks who are not subscribers to such movements also evidence advanced stages of Nigrescence, suggesting that nationalist and multicultural tendencies—while somewhat divergent—may not be incompatible. Cross (1995) concludes: "The sense of Blackness is either muted or missing at Pre-Encounter, becomes an obsession during Immersion-Emersion, and continues as a singular concern (Black Nationalism) or a concern mingled with other concerns (biculturalism or multiculturalism) at Internalization" (p. 119).

In conclusion, research over the last 20 years has shown that Black identity development is less about change in mental health status personality and more about a resocialization experience in which values, primary reference group, and degree of salience to race is undergoing change. As mentioned earlier, the Cross model was one of the first attempts in the psychological literature at theorizing about racial identity development through the use of a stage model. Though focused exclusively on Blacks, it became over the years the stepping stone for the identity development models of other racial and minority groups. Implicit in the Cross and other models of minority identity development is the assumption that such identity develops in response to an oppressive dominant society (Rowe, Bennett, & Atkinson, 1994). It is for this reason that considerable space is dedicated to the Cross model, which will be followed by an examination of subsequent models of racial/cultural identity development.

WHITE RACIAL IDENTITY

Prior to 1984, when Janet Helms's model of White Racial Identity Development (WRID) appeared, little if any consideration in the professional literature had been given to "how the condition of being White influences Whites' psychosocial development" (Helms, 1990a, p. 4). By and large, Whites are not accustomed to reflecting upon their identification to a particular racial group (White supremacists may be an exception). Still today, in many parts of the United States, a White person can go through life with little if any contact with non-Whites. This racial isolation permits many Whites to be oblivious to issues of race and racial identity.

The Helms Model of White Racial Identity Development (WRID)

Helms's (1984, 1990a, 1995) model, perhaps the most well-known and researched, assumes that Whites go through stages of racial identity development similar to those of Blacks and other minorities. Underlying the stages are two fundamental processes: the abandonment of racism and the development of a positive White racial identity. Implicit in the model is that racism is associated with a negative White racial identity leading to Helms's assertion that racism produces harmful effects to the perpetrator as well as the victim. In the original model (Helms, 1984), there were three stages associated with the abandonment of racism (contact, disintegration, and reintegration) and two with development of a positive White racial identity (pseudoindependence and autonomy). More recently (Helms, 1990a), a stage was added between pseudoindependence and autonomy, called immersion/emersion, reflecting the possibility "for Whites to seek out accurate information about their historical, political, and cultural contributions to the world, and that the process of self-examination within this context is an important component of the process of defining a positive White identity" (Helms, 1990a, p. 55). The following is a list and brief description of the six stages associated with Helms's theory of White racial identity development. The reader is to keep in mind that the identity attitudes of Whites in this model are fostered through a relationship exclusively with Blacks. Helms does not extrapolate to other non-White groups.

Contact. Whites in this stage are by and large oblivious to issues of race and racial identification. They are fond of saying that race doesn't matter to them; are unaware of how being White has benefited them; and have minimal contact with Blacks but allow themselves some socialization with those "who don't act Black." Affectively, contact Whites are generally quite content with their racial identity, avoiding any potentially anxiety-arousing situations that involve contact with Blacks. Whites at this stage are for the most part strong maintainers of the status quo. Length of time in the contact stage depends on whether the person continues to rely on vicarious—or begins to consider first-hand—information about Blacks. If the latter becomes more frequent, the person will move more quickly out of the contact stage because personal and sustained contact with the Black population will lead to self-acknowledged differences between the two groups.

Disintegration. Here, beliefs and attitudes of the contact stage are dismantled. The disintegrated White person no longer enjoys a comfortable existence easily compartmentalizing both groups. The experience of racism toward Blacks results in questioning his or her allegiance to Whites. However, not being Black, Whites at this stage feel lost, helpless, anxious, and even guilt ridden. According to Helms, disintegrated Whites inevitably will do something to reduce this state of conflict. This may take the form of avoiding contact with Blacks, convincing other Whites about the noninferiority of Blacks, or convincing themselves that racism does not exist or at least it's not their fault (Helms, 1990a). More than likely, disintegrated Whites will be drawn to the comfort of acceptance of their own racial group and become coconspirators in either overt or covert White superiority.

Reintegration. For the first time, a defined racial identity is achieved based on the clear belief and attitude that Whites are superior and Blacks are inferior. These beliefs may be expressed passively or actively. A reintegrated White who makes a concerted effort to avoid Blacks may be said to be functioning in a passive mode. Active reintegration would take the form of overt hostile and violent acts against Blacks. In a White-dominated society, it is quite easy to remain fixated at the reintegration phase. Like the move from previous stages, reintegrated Whites must undergo some painful or insightful encounter through which they question this particular definition of Whiteness.

Pseudoindependence. At this stage, the person begins to abandon the White identity achieved in the reintegration phase, however finds it difficult to forge a new identity. At best, there is an intellectual acceptance of Blacks and an acknowledgment of existing racism. Unable to locate positive White identity models, pseudoindependents initiate contact with Blacks, wanting to help by imposing White standards and White culture. Thus, they still perpetuate racism but in a more subtle fashion than in the previous stage of development. For the pseudoindependent White, the solution to racism lies in changing Blacks not Whites. Comfortable in neither the status quo White society nor the marginal Black one, this person struggles with a true White identity. The quest for a better definition of Whiteness signals the person's entry into the immersion/emersion stage.

Immersion/Emersion. At this stage, a positive White racial identity is being formed. This person dedicates more time to learning about being White, the consequences of being White, and his or her relationship to the rest of society. The focus is no longer on changing Blacks but the goal becomes changing Whites. Affectively, the person begins to relish in this new-found identity of being White, accepts it, and understands its role in the abandonment of and fight against racism.

Autonomy. The autonomy stage of White racial identity represents a continuation and solidification of the identity process begun in the immersion/emersion stage. Feeling quite comfortable with their Whiteness, Whites expand their sensitivity to other forms of oppression besides that of racism against Blacks. Autonomous Whites begin to welcome contact with diverse cultural groups and understand such contact as a mutually enriching encounter. As such, the autonomy stage of development is a never-ending process according to Helms. For the autonomous White, every racial and cultural variable is perceived as a challenging and potentially enriching experience. Coupled with the fact that at this stage of development Whites actively seek such contact, the result is a perpetual growth in their own racial identities and the experience of those who are non-White.

White Racial Consciousness Development (WRCD)

Recently, a new and different model of White racial development has emerged critiquing previous models. White racial consciousness development (Rowe, Behrens, & Leach, 1995; Rowe, Bennett, & Atkinson, 1994) takes exception to previous models that assume that Whites follow a pattern similar to the identity development of non-whites. Non-Whites are forced to develop their racial identity in response to negative stereotypes held by the dominant society and often seen as oppressive. Whites, on the other hand, develop their identity under a very different set of circumstances. "Attitudes that most Whites develop about their own group and other racial/ethnic groups are reinforced by the stereotypes of the dominant society. Thus, the system of oppression impacts the racial attitudes of both Whites and racial/ethnic minority persons, but is experienced differently" (Rowe, Bennett, & Atkinson, 1994, p. 131). Furthermore, these authors suggest that the WRID model does not really measure attitudes toward Whiteness but the attitudes of Whites toward Blacks and other racial/ethnic minorities. These attitudes of Whites towards non-Whites ought not to be confused with White racial identity. This leads to the particular critique of the Helms model by Rowe, Bennett, and Atkinson (1994), which focuses exclusively on attitudes of the dominant society toward Blacks and does not consider other non-White populations.

White racial consciousness is divided into two statuses: unachieved racial consciousness and achieved racial consciousness. Unachieved racial consciousness includes the avoidant, dependent, and dissonant types; achieved racial consciousness includes the dominative, conflictive, reactive, and integrative types. Both statuses and types represent a set of cognitive beliefs resulting in attitudes of Whites toward non-Whites. Such attitudes are not treated as representative of an underlying White identity (as in the Helms model) but rather as a state of consciousness toward those who are different racially and/or ethnically. The use of the word "type" refers not to a configuration of personality but to an attitude evidenced by a White person. All the types under achieved status indicate an exploration and commitment to racial issues and concerns, whereas in each of the types under unachieved status there is lacking either exploration or commitment or both. However, the difference between "type" models and the previously examined "stage" models is that the latter are more developmental and fluid in nature whereas the former imply more stable traits (Helms, 1990a).

The following are brief descriptions of the three types of unachieved white racial consciousness.

Avoidant Type. Attitudes of this type reflect a lack of both commitment and exploration regarding racial/ethnic minority issues. Borrowing the Cross terminology, there is a very low degree of salience for racial issues. The preferred method of dealing with any kind of racial problem or incident is avoidance, minimalization, or denial.

Dependent Type. White people of this type have committed themselves to a set of attitudes and beliefs about racial/ethnic minorities—

but without any exploration. They have not internalized such attitudes but simply adopted them either from significant others (e.g., parents), the media, or the like. They have not explored deeply why they have the beliefs they have.

Dissonant Type. People of this type are engaged in exploration, but without commitment. Commitment to previously held attitudes may have been shaken due to new experiences, resulting in confusion and uncertainty regarding their attitudes toward minority groups. They are in transition.

The following are brief descriptions of the four types of achieved White racial consciousness.

Dominative Type. Attitudes here are reflective of White supremacy. People of this type clearly understand *Whites* as superior to other racial groups and can be overtly or covertly hostile toward such groups. They see racial/ethnic minorities as less deserving than Whites and tend to see the social and economic problems of minority groups in terms of intrinsic qualities as opposed to historical disadvantage.

Conflictive Type. On the one hand, people with these attitudes are very supportive of equality among the races and supportive of legislation that promotes such. On the other hand, they are reluctant to support programs such as affirmative action or any other program that appears to promote minority groups at the expense of Whites. Though they are careful to avoid the appearance of even latent racism, they nevertheless have a greater affinity to Whites and Whiteness than to racial minority groups.

Reactive Type. Whites with reactive attitudes are very supportive of minority causes and may lead to overidentification and romanticization of a particular group. They either are, or consider themselves, alienated from the mainstream White community because of their ardent support of minority racial groups. In direct contrast to the dominative type, they overemphasize the historical antecedents for the oppression of minority groups and dismiss any kind of personal responsibility. Even the most vilified behaviors are seen as a form of survival and the result of societal oppression. Though well meaning, they sometimes adopt a paternalistic stance toward oppressed groups. On a more passive level, they represent an intellectually supportive commitment and exploration of racial minority concerns. Affectively, they are angry at White society and all those who support the status quo.

Integrative Type. At this level of consciousness, Whites accept and feel comfortable with their Whiteness, have a pluralist view of the world, and have an understanding of the sociopolitical forces affecting minority groups. The integrative type is neither angry nor guilty, with no need to oppress or idealize (Rowe, Bennett, & Atkinson, 1994). Commitment to social change can range from contributing to organizations to actively organizing and participating in demonstrations and/or movements against oppression.

WRCD and WRID Compared and Contrasted

Rowe, Bennett, and Atkinson's (1994) assertion that the WRCD model is superior to Helms's WRID model provoked a reaction by Block and Carter (1996). Though the authors of the WRCD model admit their types of White racial consciousness are similar to the stages of the WRID, they maintain that the WRID basically follows a developmental sequence. "We see movement between the statuses and types of White racial consciousness as not necessarily sequential or predictable, but a variable consequence of life experiences" (Rowe, Bennett, & Atkinson, 1994, p. 142). Interestingly, Helms, in response to the common assumption that the WRID is a strong stage model, has replaced the term *stages* with *statuses*—indicating that she always intended the stages of the WRID to be permeable (Helms, 1995).

> Draguns (personal communication, 1993) convinced me that my original use of *stages* was congruent with Freud's epigenic principle. Accordingly, resolutions of the developmental issues of earlier or more primitive stages leave their imprint on subsequent stages. Consequently, stages represent interactive themes rather than mutually exclusive categories. (Helms, 1995, p. 183)

A generic problem with developmental models is the temptation to use them categorically and simplistically. Rather than a person moving from and to a stage of development, a more appropriate consideration is the movement in and out of stages. Harkening back to our own theoretical model of situational hierarchy, this movement in and out of stages (or statuses) will depend on situations (contexts) determining the degree of racial salience. For example, a pseudoindependent or autonomous White, the product of a diversity-exposed upbringing and education, might move into a disintegrated or reintegrated stage when job hunting and confronted with affirmative action and quota policies of hiring practices in certain institutions.

Block and Carter (1996) appear to be correct when they fail to see a significant theoretical distinction between racial consciousness and racial identity in that both refer to how one views self and others. With Helms's (1995) clarification that her model is better described using statuses as opposed to stages, the criticism of its linearity is severely diminished. Furthermore, the WRCD and WRID both posit movement from a lack of awareness or consideration for being White to the development of a White racial identity ranging from White supremacist attitudes to inclusive, multicultural attitudes. Regarding the criticism that the WRID is based on a model of Black minority development, Block and Carter (1996) refute this—saying that Helms (1984) maintains that the racial identity process is different for Whites since they, unlike Blacks, can choose their environments. This choice allows them to remain more easily fixated at a particular developmental status.

Finally, White racial identity has generated considerable thought, research, and dialogue in the field of counseling. This is an indication of both its tremendous importance as a construct in multicultural counseling and the enormous influence of Helms's work. She has created fertile soil for the ongoing empirical investigation of White racial identity and its continuing theoretical evolvement and refinement. The fact that the majority of counselors in this country are White makes necessary the continued reflection on White identity. The option exists for choosing one model over another. However, White counselors cannot choose to disregard the reflection and growth concerning how they relate to their Whiteness nor can they ignore how their non-White clients relate to their own cultural identity.

MINORITY IDENTITY DEVELOPMENT MODELS

After the appearance of the Black and White identity development models, other models of minority identity development began to proliferate. To list a few: Ruiz (1990) developed an identity model for Latinos; Downing and Roush (1985) for females; Troiden (1989) for homosexuals; Poston (1990) along with Kerwin and Ponterotto (1995) for biracial persons; Ford (1987) and Atkinson, Morton, and Sue (1998) for racial/ethnic groups in general; and Reynolds and Pope (1991) for those who are members of multiple minority groups. Though it is beyond the scope of this book to examine all of these, the Atkinson, Morton, and Sue (1998) model merits some attention as it can be applied to all minority groups and their relationship to the dominant culture.

A Generic Cultural Identity Development (CID) Model

Atkinson, Morton, and Sue (1998) outlined five stages of nondominant culture identity development. Though called by different names, the stages are similar to those of the Black identity models examined earlier.

Conformity. Similar to the pre-encounter stage of the Cross (1971) model of Nigrescence, in this stage the minority person assumes a naive acceptance of and preference for the dominant culture's values. There exists a depreciation of one's own culture and cultural group and an idealization of the dominant culture. This depreciating attitude extends to other minority groups as well, yet those groups appearing more similar to the White majority are viewed more favorably (Sue & Sue, 1990).

Dissonance. At this stage, minority group members begin to question the negatively held stereotypes about their own minority group. Experience leads to questioning the uncritical assimilation of dominant culture and an appreciation of one's own nondominant culture (Gushue, 1993). As in the encounter stage of the Cross (1971) model and the disintegration stage of the Helms (1990a) model of the WRID, this person suffers from very conflictual attitudes of appreciation and depreciation toward self and others from both dominant and nondominant groups.

Resistance. Much as in the resistance stage of the Nigrescence model, a person at this stage evidences guilt, shame, and anger at the dominant White society for having been co-opted by White values and having denigrated his or her own cultural background. Thus, the attitude toward self and members of one's minority group is appreciating while the attitude toward the dominant group is depreciating. The attitude toward other minority groups is ambivalent, resulting from the conflict between culturo-centrism (very strong at this stage of development) and empathic feelings for other minority groups who also are seen suffocating from the oppression of White culture.

Introspection. At this stage, minority people begin to question their ethnocentric basis for judging themselves and others. The self-identity derived in the resistance stage from a reaction against Whites begins to be replaced by a more positive self-identity, more proactive than reactive. There is no longer the unequivocal appreciation of one's own group, as the individual in the introspection stage is free enough to criticize aspects of his or her own cultural group that are oppressive and nonliberating. At the same time, this individual feels conflicted around the global damnation of White culture while having positive encounters with Whites.

Integrative Awareness. This final stage of identity development involves a true appreciation for one's own culture and selective appreciation of White culture. There is a deep belief that there are desirable and nondesirable elements in all cultural groupings. A critical interest and pride in one's own culture is accompanied by a critical acceptance of White culture. However, this person continues to resist political marginalization and cultural assimilation to the mainstream (Gushue, 1993).

The reader will notice quite easily the similarity between the CID model of minorities and the Black identity development models. To be more inclusive, it may be helpful to see White and Black identity development as metaphors for dominant and nondominant culture identity development. The interaction of these two cultural groupings based on an unequal share of political, economic, and social power is responsible for the attitudes associated with the different stages of development. Racial identity models are expandable to cultural identity models, which in turn are inclusive of all relationships in which the participants differ in power and status. Feminist identity development (Downing & Roush, 1985; McNamara & Rickard, 1989) and gay identity development (Cass, 1979; Pope, 1995; Troiden, 1979, 1989) models, to mention only two minority groups among others, follow much the same scheme as the CID model.

MEASUREMENT OF RACIAL/CULTURAL IDENTITY DEVELOPMENT

Over the last 15 years, numerous instruments have been created to operationalize the stages of racial/cultural identity development.

Measuring Black Racial Identity

The Racial Identity Attitude Scale (RIAS), developed by Parham and Helms (1981), was the first attempt to operationalize the Cross model of Nigrescence. Developed on Black female and male college student samples, the RIAS consists of 30 items designed to measure the *predominating* racial attitude of an individual, since it is hypothesized that all have some of each attitude. Thus, the RIAS allows for use of scores on all four subscales (note: the scale does not operationalize the fifth stage of the Cross model, internalization/commitment) with higher scores, indicating predominance of a particular racial attitude. Internal consistency reliability coefficients for the RIAS range from .66 to .77 (Parham & Helms, 1981). Ponterotto and Wise (1987) conducted a factor analytic study of the RIAS that supported the existence of all the RIAS stages except for the encounter stage.

Two other versions of the RIAS exist: the RIAS-B (short form) (Helms, 1990b) and the RIAS-B (long form) (Helms & Parham, 1990). The RIAS-B (short form) consists of the same 30 items as the original RIAS but with some items assigned to different subscales. Reported scale reliabilities for the RIAS-B (short form) are .69 (preencounter), .50 (encounter), .67 (immersion/emersion), and .79 (internalization) (Helms,

1990b). The RIAS-L consists of 50 items, 30 from the original RIAS and 20 newly designed items. The RIAS-L also redistributes some of the original items. Fischer, Tokar, and Serna (1998) conducted a validation study on the RIAS-L using 275 Black college students and community members. Three of the four RIAS-L subscales had coefficient alphas of .70 or higher; however, the encounter subscale was at .43. The low internal consistency for the encounter stage concurs with previous studies and places an upper limit on its validity (Fischer, Tokar, & Serna, 1998). The RIAS-L promises to be the most widely used instrument for future research on Black racial identity, therefore necessitating more investigation into its psychometric properties.

Measuring White Racial Identity

Presently, there exist two measures of White racial identity stemming from the two different theories about Whiteness that were articulated earlier, namely the White Racial Identity Attitude Scale (WRIAS) (Helms & Carter, 1990) and the recently developed Oklahoma Racial Attitudes Scale: Preliminary Form (ORAS-P) (Choney & Behrens, 1996). A third, the White Racial Consciousness Development Scale (WRCDS) (Claney & Parker, 1989), has received less attention in the literature, and data suggest that it lacks adequate reliability and concurrent validity (Choney & Rowe, 1994).

WRIAS. This consists of 60 attitudinal statements using a 5-point Likert scale designed to measure the six stages of Helms's (1984) theory of White racial identity. Consistent with the theory, items measure attitudes about Whites and Blacks since together the attitudes about both contribute to one's racial identity. The WRIAS has been widely used since its availability both in published research studies (Choney & Rowe, 1994; Neville, Heppner, Louie, Thompson, Brooks, & Baker, 1996; Ottavi, Pope-Davis, & Dings, 1994; Tokar & Swanson, 1991) and numerous unpublished doctoral dissertations. Helms and Carter (1990) reported internal consistency (alpha) coefficients as .55 (contact), .77 (disintegration), .80 (reintegration), .71 (pseudoindependence), and .67 (autonomy). Construct validity studies on the WRIAS have shown it to be predictive of racist attitudes

(Pope-Davis & Ottavi, 1994) and multicultural counseling competence (Ottavi, Pope-Davis, & Dings, 1994). Some studies (Ottavi, Pope-Davis, & Dings, 1994; Pope-Davis, Dings, Stone, & Vandiver, 1995; Pope-Davis, Menefee, & Ottavi, 1993) have indicated high correlations among the subscales, which have led some to question the multidimensionality of the WRIAS and to suggest that it is more a bipolar measure of general racism (Behrens, 1997; Rowe, Behrens, & Leach, 1995).

ORAS-P. The Oklahoma Racial Attitudes Scale (ORAS-P) (Choney & Behrens, 1996) is designed to measure White racial consciousness theory (Rowe, Bennett, & Atkinson, 1994). The ORAS-P consists of 42 items: 10 representing the unachieved status types, 31 items related to the achieved status types, and one item that is not scored (Leach, 1996). Each item is scored according to a 5-point Likert scale format from "strongly agree" to "strongly disagree." Initial analyses of the ORAS-P were conducted on samples of undergraduate students in psychology and educational psychology at the University of Oklahoma. Though the development of this scale is in its infant stages, preliminary data regarding the integrity of the scales and their relationship appear highly consistent. Leach (1996) reported Cronbach's alphas ranging from .68 (avoidant) to .82 (dependent). Test-retest reliabilities during a 4-week interval ranged from .46 (dissonant) to .76 (reactive). However, the developers of the ORAS-P admit quite readily that much more work is needed on the scale before it is available for general use. Nevertheless, alongside of the WRIAS, the ORAS-P appears to be the only other promising instrument for measuring White racial attitudes.

RACIAL/CULTURAL IDENTITY DEVELOPMENT AND THE COUNSELING RELATIONSHIP

In her seminal article on Black and White identity development, Helms (1984) classified four possible relationship types between a White counselor and a Black client (or vice versa): parallel, progressive, regressive, and crossed. A parallel relationship is one in which client and counselor are at the same level of identity. For example, a White client at the contact stage and a Black client at the preencounter stage would be in a parallel relationship. A progressive relationship is defined as the counselor's being at least one level higher than the client. A White counselor at the pseudoindependent stage with a Black client at the encounter stage would enjoy a progressive relationship. A regressive relationship is defined as the counselor's being at least one level lower than the client. A White counselor at the reintegration stage with a Black client at the internalization stage would be a regressive relationship. Finally, a crossed relationship is one in which the participants have directly opposite attitudes. For example, a Black person at the internalization stage—pro-Black/neutral White is in a crossed relationship with a White person at the pseudoindependent stage—pro-White/neutral Black.

The hypothesis quite obviously is that progressive relationships are beneficial to the counseling process while regressive relationships are detrimental. The Helms process model has received empirical support in the literature (Bradby & Helms, 1990; Carter, 1988, 1990; Carter & Helms, 1992; Helms & Carter, 1991). An in-depth, applied examination of dominant and nondominant interaction models will take place in the second half of this book. Because of empirical support for the Helms theory, even in its application to the counseling process, I believe that it has the most clinical utility in spite of its ongoing evolution.

The assessment of identity status within a counseling framework can take place formally and informally. The instruments discussed earlier for measuring racial cultural identity development are designed primarily for research purposes. However, Helms (1992) has developed a measure of racial statuses for use with groups and consciousness-raising workshops. A more informal assessment can take place as the counselor listens for racial identity themes when matters of race and culture are being discussed. With the developmental status model in mind, the counselor can qualitatively assess a client's racial identity status. For assessment purposes, counselors can ask a minority client: "How do you relate to (or deal with) being…in a White-dominated society?" Hopefully, the day will arrive when counselors can ask White clients: "How do you relate to being White?" without such a question seeming ludicrous. Just as counselors ask clients during an intake assessment about the relationship with their mother and father, they should consider it no less important to ask about clients' relationship to their own race.

SUMMARY

Identity development, almost by the very nature of the concept, is articulated through stage models. The inherent danger of stage models is the implicit invitation to label and categorize in strict fashion. We saw earlier how Helms (1995) changed the word stage to "statuses" in an attempt to imbue her model with more fluidity. Ironically, racial/cultural identity development models originated to heighten sensitivity to intragroup differences among cultural groups and to avoid stereotyping. It would be sad if such models created the very problem they were trying to obviate. Therefore, it is very important that counselors use these models as guides, as one of many other metaphors attempting to understand the experiences of culturally diverse clients, and that the various stages of identity be seen more as "statuses" into and from which individuals can move in and out, depending on a variety of situational variables. Though one status may dominate, individuals are challenged every day by internal and external events to reconsider who they are, their attitudes toward themselves and others. It is within this mindset that cultural identity development models should be incorporated into the counseling relationship and process.

REFERENCES

Atkinson, D.R., Morton, G., & Sue, D.W. (1998). *Counseling American minorities*. Boston: McGraw-Hill.

Behrens, J.T. (1997). Does the White Racial Identity Attitude Scale measure racial identity? *Journal of Counseling Psychology, 44,* 3–12.

Block, C.J., & Carter, R.T. (1996). White racial identity attitude theories: A rose by any other name is still a rose. *The Counseling Psychologist, 24,* 326–334.

Bradby, D., & Helms, J.E. (1990). Black racial identity attitudes and White therapist cultural sensitivity in cross-racial therapy dyads: An exploratory study. In J.E. Helms (Ed.), *Black and White racial identity: Theory, research, and practice*. Westport, CT: Greenwood.

Carter, R.T. (1988). An empirical test of a theory on the influence of racial identity attitudes on the counseling process within a workshop setting. (Doctoral dissertation, University of Maryland, 1987.) *Dissertation Abstracts International, 49,* 431–A.

Carter, R.T. (1990). Does race or racial identity attitudes influence the counseling process in Black and White dyads? In J.E. Helms (Ed.), *Black and White racial identity: Theory, research, and practice* (pp. 145–163). Westport, CT: Greenwood.

Carter, R.T., & Helms, J.E. (1992). The counseling process as defined by relationship types: A test of Helms's interactional model. *Journal of Multicultural Counseling and Development, 20,* 181–201.

Cass, V.C. (1979). Homosexual identity formation: A theoretical model. *Journal of Homosexuality, 4,* 219–235.

Choney, S.K., & Behrens, J.T. (1996). Development of the Oklahoma Racial Attitudes Scale—Preliminary Form (ORAS-P). In G.R. Sodowsky & J. Impara (Eds.), *Multicultural assessment in counseling and clinical psychology* (pp. 225–240). Lincoln, NE: Buros Institute of Mental Measurements.

Choney, S.K., & Rowe, W. (1994). Assessing White racial identity: The White Racial Consciousness Development Scale (WRCDS). *Journal of Counseling and Development, 73,* 102–104.

Claney, D., & Parker, W.M. (1989). Assessing White racial consciousness and perceived comfort with Black individuals: A preliminary study. *Journal of Counseling and Development, 67,* 449–451.

Cross, W.E. (1971). The Negro-to-Black conversion experience. *Black World, 20,* 13–27.

Cross, W.E. (1995). The psychology of Nigrescence. In J.G. Ponterotto, J.M. Casas, L.A. Suzuki, & C.M. Alexander (Eds.), *Handbook of multicultural counseling* (pp. 93–122). Thousand Oaks, CA: Sage.

Cross, W.E., Parham, T.A., & Helms, J.E. (1991). The stages of Black identity development: Nigresence models. In R.L. Jones (Ed.), *Black psychology* (3rd ed., pp. 319–338). Hampton, VA: Cobb & Henry.

Downing, N.E., & Roush, K.L. (1985). From passive acceptance to active commitment: A model of feminist identity for women. *The Counseling Psychologist, 13,* 695–709.

Fischer, A.R., Tokar, D.M., & Serna, G.S. (1998). Validity and construct contamination of the Racial Identity Attitude Scale—Long Form. *Journal of Counseling Psychology, 45,* 212–224.

Ford, D.Y., Harris, J., & Schuerger, J.M. (1993). Racial identity development among gifted Black students: Counseling issues and concerns. *Journal of Counseling and Development, 71,* 409–417.

Ford, R.C. (1987). Cultural awareness and cross-cultural counseling. *International Journal for the Advancement of Counseling, 10,* 71–78.

Gushue, G.V. (1993). Cultural identity development and family assessment: An interaction model. *The Counseling Psychologist, 21,* 487–513.

Helms, J.E. (1984). Toward a theoretical explanation of the effects of race on counseling. A Black and White model. *The Counseling Psychologist, 13,* 695–710.

Helms, J.E., (Ed.). (1990a). *Black and White racial identity: Theory, research, and practice.* Westport, CT: Greenwood.

Helms, J.E. (1990b). The measurement of Black racial identity attitudes. In J.E. Helms (Ed.), *Black and White racial identity: Theory, research, and practice* (pp. 31–47). Westport, CT: Greenwood Press.

Helms, J.E., (1992). *A race is a nice thing to have.* Topeka, KS: Content Communications.

Helms, J.E. (1995). An update of Helms's White and people of color racial identity models. In J.G. Ponterotto, J.M. Casas, L.A. Suzuki, & C.M. Alexander (Eds.), *Handbook of multicultural counseling* (pp. 181–198). Thousand Oaks, CA: Sage.

Helms, J.E., & Carter, R.T. (1990). Development of the White racial identity inventory. In J.E. Helms (Ed.), *Black and white racial identity: Theory, research, and practice* (pp. 67–80). Westport, CT: Greenwood Press.

Helms, J.E., & Carter, R.T. (1991). Relationships of White and Black racial identity attitudes and demographic similarity to counselor preferences. *Journal of Counseling Psychology, 38,* 446–457.

Helms, J.E., & Parham, T.A. (1990). The relationship between Black racial identity attitudes and cognitive styles. In J.E. Helms (Ed.), *Black and White racial identity: Theory, research, and practice* (pp. 119–131). Westport, CT: Greenwood Press.

Helms, J.E., & Parham, T.A. (1996). The development of the Racial Identity Attitude Scale. In R.L. Jones (Ed.), *Handbook of tests and measurements for Black populations* (Vol. 2, pp. 167–174). Hampton, VA: Cobb & Henry.

Hoare, C.H. (1991). Psychosocial identity development and cultural others. *Journal of Counseling and Development, 70,* 45–53.

Kerwin, C., & Ponterotto, J.G. (1995). Biracial identity development: Theory and research. In J.G. Ponterotto, J.M. Casas, L.A. Suzuki, & C.M. Alexander (Eds.), *Handbook of multicultural counseling* (pp. 199–217). Thousand Oaks, CA: Sage.

Leach, M.M. (1996, August). Measuring White racial consciousness: Developing the Oklahoma Racial Attitudes Scale. In J.M. Casas (Chair), *White racial identity and White racial consciousness: Meeting the challenge.* Symposium conducted at the annual meeting of the American Psychological Association, Toronto, Canada.

McNamara, K., & Rickard, K.M. (1989). Feminist identity development: Implications for feminist therapy with women. *Journal of Counseling and Development, 68,* 184–189.

Neville, H.A., Heppner, M.J., Louie, C.E., Thompson, D.E., Brooks, L., & Baker, C.E. (1996). The impact of multicultural training on White racial identity attitudes and therapy competencies. *Professional Psychology: Research and Practice, 27,* 83–89.

Ottavi, T.M., Pope-Davis, D.B., & Dings, J.G. (1994). Relationship between White racial identity attitudes and self-reported multicultural counseling competencies. *Journal of Counseling Psychology, 41,* 149–154.

Parham, T.A. (1989). Cycles of psychological Nigrescence. *The Counseling Psychologist, 17,* 187–226.

Parham, T.A., & Helms, J.E. (1981). The influence of Black students' racial identity attitudes on preferences for counselor's race. *Journal of Counseling Psychology, 28,* 250–257

Ponterotto, J.G., & Wise, S.L. (1987). Construct validity study of the Racial Identity Attitude Scale. *Journal of Counseling Psychology, 34,* 218–223.

Pope, M. (1995). The "salad bowl" is big enough for us all: An argument for the inclusion of lesbians and gay men in any definition of multiculturalism. *Journal of Counseling and Development, 73,* 301–304.

Pope-Davis, D.B., Dings, J., Stone, G.L., & Vandiver, B. 1995, August). *White racial identity attitude development: A comparison of two instruments.* Paper presented at the 103rd Annual Convention of the American Psychological Association, New York, NY.

Pope-Davis, D.B., Menefee, L.A., & Ottavi, T.M. (1993). The comparison of White racial identity attitudes among faculty and students: Implications for professional psychologists. *Professional Psychology: Research and Practice, 24,* 443–449.

Pope-Davis, D.B., & Ottavi, T.M. (1994). The relationship between racism and racial identity among White Americans. *Journal of Counseling and Development, 72,* 316–322.

Poston, W.S. (1990). The biracial identity development model: A needed addition. *Journal of Counseling and Development, 69,* 152–159.

Reynolds, A.L., & Pope, R.L. (1991). The complexities of diversity. Exploring multiple oppressions. *Journal of Counseling and Development, 70,* 174–180.

Rowe, W., Behrens, J.T., & Leach, M.M. (1995). Racial ethnic identity and racial consciousness. In J.G. Ponterotto, J.M. Casas, L.A. Suzuki, & C.M. Alexander (Eds.), *Handbook of multicultural counseling* (pp. 218–235). Thousand Oaks, CA: Sage.

Rowe, W., Bennett, S.K., and Atkinson, D.R. (1994). White racial identity models: A critique and alternative proposal. *The Counseling Psychologist, 22,* 129–146.

Ruiz, A.S. (1990). Ethnic identity: Crisis and resolution. *Journal of Multicultural Counseling and Development, 18,* 29–40.

Sue, D.W. & Sue, D. (1990). *Counseling the culturally different: Theory and Practice.* New York: John Wiley & Sons.

Tokar, D.M., & Swanson, J.L. (1991). An investigation of the validity of Helms's (1984) model of White racial identity development. *Journal of Counseling Psychology, 38,* 296–301.

Troiden, R.R. (1979). Becoming homosexual. A model of gay identity acquisition. *Psychiatry, 42,* 362–373.

Troiden, R.R. (1989). The formation of homosexual identities. *Journal of Homosexuality, 17,* 43–73.

PART II

—~∿∿~—

Multiculturalism: Across Counseling Modalities

Part II of this book is about integrating the constructs of second-culture acquisition and cultural identity development across different counseling modalities, namely, individual, group, family, and organizational counseling. These four modalities constitute the four chapters in this section, all of which are organized in the same fashion. The first part of each chapter introduces the reader to more traditional counseling principles specific to the modality under discussion. These principles are then discussed as to their relevance and appropriateness to counseling from a multicultural perspective. Each of these chapters ends with a lengthy case example that integrates the material previously discussed.

The organization of these chapters represents my position on multicultural counseling. Rather than a radical rejection of all traditional counseling as representative of White Eurocentrism and therefore useless in a multicultural approach, this book allows for an integrationist perspective. As discussed in Chapter 1, there are some counseling principles (even more traditional ones) and core conditions that are of an etic quality and transcend culture. While others disagree, seeing even core conditions as discriminatory, Weinrach and Thomas (1998) rightly point out that no one theory of multicultural counseling has emerged over the last 20 years. Rather, all counseling theories, approaches, strategies, and so forth are to be held accountable and scrutinized for their appropriateness to culturally diverse populations (Pederson, 1996). These chapters intend to do what Pederson recommends—first by articulating some of the traditional approaches in a particular modality and then by refining and integrating them into a multicultural perspective.

REFERENCES

Pederson, P. (1996). The importance of both similarities and differences in multicultural counseling: Reaction to Patterson. *Journal of Counseling and Development, 74,* 236–237.

Weinrach, S.G., & Thomas, K.R. (1998). Diversity-sensitive counseling today: A postmodern clash of values. *Journal of Counseling and Development, 76,* 115–122.

—⌒∿∿⌒—

CHAPTER 4

INDIVIDUAL MULTICULTURAL COUNSELING

FUNDAMENTAL PRINCIPLES IN INDIVIDUAL COUNSELING

Reducing to several pages the fundamentals of counseling, whose history and development span more than half a century, is a daunting challenge. The approach is basically eclectic and the material is the result primarily of my own counseling experience and secondarily of having read the more well-known and utilized texts on counseling. What follows is not an exhaustive list of counseling principles but more an introduction to, and overview of, individual counseling with an eye toward integrating these principles into a multiculturally sensitive perspective.

Development of the Working Alliance

Regardless of theoretical orientation, a trusting relationship between counselor and client is essential for any effective work to be accomplished (Cormier & Cormier, 1990; Doyle, 1992; Egan, 1998; Meier & Davis, 1997). However, theoretical orientation will determine the degree of importance associated with the working alliance. For example, a strict behaviorist will place less emphasis on the relationship than will a Rogerian. The former considers the working alliance as a necessary means through which techniques can be effectively assigned to the client, while the latter considers counseling to be the relationship. However, in spite of such differences, the counseling profession has relied on the so-called "microskills" to develop the working alliance. These skills are briefly reviewed and then examined critically from a diversity perspective.

Counseling Microskills

What follows is an overview of microskills based on importance as determined by both my experience and the confluence of classic texts on counseling.

Attending Behaviors. These behaviors refer to the way counselors use their bodies to communicate a genuine interest in the client. Attending behaviors include posture, eye contact, and degree of relaxation. Egan (1998) uses the acronym *SOLER* (square, open, leaning, eye contact, and relaxed) to summarize effective attending behaviors. Good attending behaviors transmit positive energy, which is crucial in the building of the working alliance.

Even attending behaviors are culturally based. For example, our dominant culture values an open posture and eye contact as signs of nondefensiveness and therefore conducive to establishing an effective counseling relationship. However, this is not true for all cultures. For example, in many Asian cultures direct eye contact is a sign of disrespect, and respect is shown by a slight lowering of the head. A relevant incident occurred during my tenure as a school counselor, when an assistant principal was screaming at an Asian student to look him in the eye when being spoken to. This insensitive and uninformed administrator did not understand that the student—because of his cultural background—actually was showing respect by not making eye contact. When doing cross-cultural, psychosocial assessments, a counselor must be careful in pathologizing nonverbal behaviors. It would be wrong for a counselor to use an Asian client's downward look as evidence for bolstering a hypothesis of depression.

Clarification. Clarification is an intervention by the counselor to gain a deeper understanding of something communicated by the client. Beginning counselors make the mistake of *assuming* they know what the client is talking about. A good counseling principle is: Assume nothing and get the client to explain what was meant. A simple example would be the client who comes to counseling and says: "I'm depressed." At this point, it would be ineffective for counselors to assume they know what the client means by "depressed" and offer an empathic remark. Rather, a clarifying response is in order such as: "Can you help me to understand what you mean when you say you are depressed?" Beginning counseling students, in my experience, have a difficult time understanding the importance of good clarifying responses. The implications of their importance are threefold: They highlight the uniqueness of each client; they help clients tell their story; and they have a cathartic effect, as the client is asked to talk of details about a problem perhaps unmentionable before the counseling encounter. The failure to ask clarifying questions is a form of avoidance on the part of the counselor and is therefore not conducive to effective counseling.

Within the multicultural perspective, the counselor employs clarification as a tool for understanding more about the client's cultural background. Rather than judge the client from the perspective of the dominant culture, the counselor can use clarification to gain a greater understanding for how clients have been shaped by their cultural background and to differentiate between what is culturally acceptable behavior and pathological behavior. I remember working with a Puerto Rican woman steeped in the tradition of *espiritismo* (spiritism), a worldview that understands one's fate in life as determined by the good and evil spirits existing outside of oneself and warring with each other. If one is having emotional difficulties or problems, it is because somehow the evil spirits have dominated the good spirits, necessitating the intervention of an *espiritista* (spiritist). This indigenous healer has the ability through various rituals to remove the influence of the evil spirits and allow the good spirits to reestablish control and influence. When my client would talk about the evil spirits controlling her, my mind would automatically resort to categories of paranoia, psychosis, external locus of control, and poor reality testing. Fortunately, I had attended recently a series of lectures on espiritismo and thus had the capacity to ask clarifying questions—not so much to confirm my traditional categories but more to confirm the worldview of es-piritismo. Later, the client agreed to my proposal that an espiritista be in-vited to work with us in helping restore the positive influences in her life. Once the client agreed, treatment became all the more successful.

The above scenario indicates the importance of counselor knowl-edge about the client's culture. The client herself was not able to explain conceptually the worldview of espiritismo. Since the counselor had some knowledge of espiritismo, he was able to ask informed, clarifying ques-tions. Without that knowledge he was most likely doomed to labeling the client with traditional categories of psychopathology. Thus, it is worth re-peating that, when working cross-culturally, the counselor has the clinical and ethical obligation to gain as much knowledge as possible about the client's cultural background. Some of this knowledge may come from clients themselves, but the counselor must go beyond the client for a more generalized and conceptualized understanding of the client's culture.

Reflection. Reflection is a microskill usually designating the counselor's attempt to give back (reflect) to clients the feeling associated with the con-tent of their story. For example, a client might say: "Everything I have tried lately has not produced any positive results," to which the counselor might respond: "It sounds like you're feeling quite frustrated because of a lot of ef-fort and no results." Reflection responses serve as a catalyst for allowing the client to experience the affect associated with a particular problem or situation. Therefore, reflection responses are used more by counselors whose theoretical orientation supports the belief that the experience and expres-sion of affect are responsible for therapeutic change and healing.

The microskill of reflection has its roots in an approach to counseling that is nondirective and emphasizes feelings. Both these dimensions must be employed with circumspection when working cross-culturally because reflecting feelings can be culturally alienating. Clients from nondominant cultures may look to counselors as experts whose role is to tell them what to do. This is a difficult situation, because the counselor must negotiate a stance between empowering the client by not replicating the dominant and nondominant dynamic pervasive in the life of a minority client and not alienating the client by assuming an absolute stance of nondirectiveness. Empowerment is not a given; it is a process. A good analogy may be to the supervisory relationship where beginning supervisees look to the supervisor for advice and direction, and assume a "tell me what to do" stance. A good supervisor will understand this developmental stage and gratify the supervisee's need while at the same time planting the seeds for a later and more collaborative stage of supervision. Something similar happens in the counseling process. Underrepresented clients who oftentimes feel powerless in so many areas of their lives very easily will assume a "tell me what to do" stance. A good counselor will recognize that some directiveness is called for and at the same time plant seeds for empowerment. In other words, a counselor can be very active and directive for the purposes of empowerment. In my work with families (to be discussed at length in Chapter 6), I was very directive, but always with the goal of empowering the parent or parents to be effective executors in the family system. In short, skilled multicultural counselors will be flexible in their degree of nondirectiveness in the counseling process but always with the understanding that counseling is a coinvestigation into alternate meanings of experience (Ivey, 1995).

The second dimension of the reflection response is the tendency to employ its use for facilitating the expression of affect on the part of the client. This emphasis is both theoretically and culturally based. The psycho analytic tradition has imprinted the notion that psychological problems are first and foremost due to repressed affect. Thus, the goal of treatment is to facilitate the expression of repressed affect. Furthermore, in some cultures emotional expression is highly valued, while in others it is seen as a sign of weakness. One is more likely to see emotional expression in Latino cultures than in Asian cultures. Thus, probing for feelings or using reflection responses with an Asian client may be culturally insensitive and very disconcerting for the client. My own recent experience has more to do with geography. As an Italian American born and brought up in New York City with a high degree of emotionality, I moved to teach in a small Southern city where I was told that students were actually scared because they found me too "intense." Informed multicultural counselors will not allow their own theoretical orientations or cultural backgrounds to determine the emphasis upon cognition or affect in the counseling process but will make the necessary adjustments based on the client's cultural background.

Probes. Probes are open-ended questions designed to elicit more information on something, or related to something, the client has communicated. The counselor can probe for thoughts, feelings, or behaviors depending on which seems more important, given the present scenario. A word of caution regarding the use of probes for feelings. The typical counselor response is: "How does that make you feel when...?" This is too banal a response and is often associated with caricatures of counselors and therapists. A better response is: "How do you react inside when...?" Probes are designed to elicit information that the counselee is unwilling to offer on his or her own accord but which the counselor thinks is relevant and important. They differ from clarifying questions because they are not necessarily about what the client has said but go beyond the client's frame of reference. For example, a mother may be talking about how difficult it is for her to allow her teenage daughter space, as they always had a very close relationship. A counselor probe could be: "Could you tell me a little bit about what life was like for you when you were your daughter's age?" Probes are important, and they facilitate a fuller version of the client's story. However, if overdone, probes allow a counseling session to take on the flavor of an interrogation.

Much of what was said about clarifying questions can be said about probes when working cross-culturally. Probes are designed to help understand clients more fully by exploring their socioculturo context. Multiculturalism—unlike more traditional foci of counseling—urges the counselor to understand how a client from a nondominant culture constructs reality. Thus, from a multicultural perspective, probes are designed to learn more about clients' culture and how it has shaped their worldview. When a client says, "In my country...," the counselor should take this as an invitation to explore further what life was like in the client's country. I worked with many immigrant parents who had been investigated because of suspicion of physical abuse toward their children. These parents resented the state's intrusion in their family life and would contrast this with how children were dealt with in their native country. Instead of immediately admonishing them as to how things are different in this country, a better approach was to explore with them parent-child relationships in their native country along with acceptable ways of disciplining and punishing children. By probing in this fashion, the problem can be reframed as one of cultural conflict, as a challenge in second-culture acquisition, and not a case of bad parents in need of monitoring by the state. This way of proceeding tends to reduce parents' hostility and resistance to changing the methods of punishing their children.

Confrontation. It might seem conceptually odd to include confrontation under the heading "Developing the Working Alliance." However, any counseling intervention that facilitates a more complete and honest elicitation of the client's story is helping to develop a working alliance. Egan (1998) prefers the term *challenge*, which has a more positive connotation than perhaps does *confrontation*. In any event, this microskill is about picking up on client contradictions that may exist between what they say and what they do, between two things they say, or between their verbal and nonverbal behavior. Few, if any, clients will come into counseling ready to tell their entire story with all its mangled parts. Some resistance is natural and even healthy at the beginning phases of counseling. Contradictions can be construed as a manifestation of such resistance, and confrontation as helping the client work through the resistance. Good confrontational responses can be constructed in the following manner: "I'm a bit confused. On the one hand...on the other hand...." The two contradictory parts of the client would fill the ellipses. Many clients do not like to be challenged, and counselors should be ready to have this intervention responded to with denial, dismissal, or minimization. However, as with most counseling interventions, more important than the intervention itself is the client's response to the intervention. A good counselor will always follow up a strong reaction by the client: "I noticed when I said...you became quite.... Is that something we can talk about?"

Summarization. Summarization is a counseling microskill that attempts to elucidate patterns of thoughts, feelings, or behaviors that are evident to the counselor after a significant amount of active listening. As such, they are powerful interventions used sparingly. Their significance can be accentuated by leaning forward and beginning the intervention with: "I've been listening for awhile, and what strikes me...." Summarization is a means for elucidating the core issue for a particular client. If the client's story can be considered analogous to a song, the counselor should be thinking: What is the refrain?

Counseling microskills, in general, serve to accomplish the first leg of the helping process: Get the client's story (Egan, 1998). There is reciprocity between the telling of one's story and the development of the working alliance. The alliance serves to facilitate the client's story, but it is also true that the telling of the story facilitates the alliance. Storytelling answers a twofold question for the counselor: Where is this client now? And where have they come from? Storytelling comes to replace the medical model—based terms of assessment and diagnosis and is a more cross-culturally sensitive way of conceptualizing the importance of truly understanding the client's uniqueness.

Empathy

Although empathy is considered by most to be another microskill in counseling, here it is given a separate section because of its overall centrality in the counseling process. Yet empathy is something that the more one tries to explain, the more elusive it becomes. The phrase "empathic understanding" implies that empathy is a particular form of understanding, and the most powerful. The following is an attempt to explain this sometimes esoteric concept.

Rogers (1959) described empathy as feeling "as if one were the other person" (p. 210). The etymology of the word *empathy* suggests a feeling in, a state of being inside another person, or adopting another's internal frame of reference (Truaff & Carkhuff, as cited in Duan & Hill, 1996). These definitions connote a sense of intimacy and closeness with another person from which is derived the power and centrality of empathy in the counseling process. Genuine empathy occurs in those rare moments when counselors truly feel they understand the client, and the client feels truly understood. To know it is to have experienced it. Over the years, I have learned to index my level of empathy for a client with my hesitancy to speak. The greater the level of empathy, the more hesitant I am to speak—knowing that words will not express the intensity of the moment.

Though empathy can be communicated through nonverbal means (body language occurring as the same energy is felt by two people), most counselors feel compelled to communicate empathy verbally. A simple "I understand how you feel" can be rather superficial. In the moments of deep and genuine empathy, the preference is for an immediacy response, for the counselors to share what is going on inside of them at that very moment. For example, a counselor might say: "Right now, I have a feeling of sadness inside of me—having listened to all that you have been through." Such moments may be rare in the counseling process, but they are the moments that give a certain sacredness and reward to the counseling profession.

Theorists argue as to whether empathy is primarily affective in nature, "responding with the same emotion to another person's emotion" (Gladstein, 1983, p. 468, as cited in Duan & Hill, 1996), or primarily cognitive, "intellectually taking the role or perspective of another person" (Gladstein, 1983, p. 468, as cited in Duan & Hill, 1996). I have always considered empathy as primarily affective in nature. However, this depends on one's own theoretical orientation, which would determine generally the primacy of affect over cognition or vice versa. Furthermore, it is argued whether empathy is a trait (some individuals are more empathic by nature or by development) or a state (some situations just naturally evoke empathy) (Duan & Hill, 1996). Empathy is too complicated and intricate a process to be defined neatly along the lines of trait versus state. For most of us, there are some clients and situations with whom it is very easy to empathize and others with whom it is very difficult. On the other hand, the challenge for counselors is to develop empathy that goes beyond a few select clients. This development has implications for multicultural counseling: the challenge of being empathic with someone whose cultural background is vastly different from one's own. This challenge is dealt with in the case example later in the chapter.

We spoke earlier of the important and challenging aspects of empathy to the counseling process. Though it is a traditional construct in counseling, the belief is that empathy is of etic proportions. The potential value of getting inside the world of another affectively and/or cognitively is not restricted by culture. However, cultural differences can restrict the capacity for empathy on the part of counselors and will depend upon their own level of racial/cultural identity development. Lower levels of counselor racial/cultural identity development will limit the capacity for cross-cultural empathy, as lower levels of identity development are associated with more closed attitudes to the culturally different. For example, White counselors at the disintegration stage will have difficulty immersing themselves in the world of a Black client and will not experience the potential enrichment of such immersion. If White and Black are metaphors for dominant and nondominant cultures, our assumptions about cross-cultural empathy can expand to counselors from dominant cultures working with clients from nondominant cultures. For example, only heterosexual counselors who have worked through their own homophobia and are in touch with their own homoerotic parts understand heterosexuality as merely one way of being in a relationship, thereby allowing them to enter the world of a homosexual client. The examples are many, but the multicultural counseling principle is one: Those counselors who have reached higher levels of racial/cultural identity development understand themselves as cultural/contextual beings entering a relationship with another cultural/contextual being for the purposes of discovering alternate meanings that are mutually enriching (Ivey, 1995). This is one dimension of cross-cultural empathy.

Aside from the counselor's own level of racial/cultural identity development as a key factor in developing empathy across cultures, there also exists the commonality of second-culture acquisition experience. Chapter 2 exposed theoretically and at length the dynamics of the acculturative experience. However, two things should remain clear about this experience: It is stressful, though the level of stress will depend on many variables, and in many instances oppressive, as those from the nondominant culture share unequally in political, economic, and social power. Furthermore, members of nondominant cultures—because they either look, act, or speak differently—suffer negative stereotypes and prejudice at the hands of the dominant culture. Thus, a crucial aspect of cross-cultural empathy is to have a felt appreciation and understanding for the social oppression experienced by the client. The counselor must be careful not to understand the possible resistance, paranoia, anxiety, and avoidance by the client as intrapsychic but more the result of societal oppression and prejudice. This kind of empathy is difficult if one has lived a privileged existence of always having enjoyed dominant cultural status. But it is important for counselors to find unique ways of developing this sort of empathy. When my caseload was predominantly Puerto Rican, I made a point of spending time in Puerto Rican neighborhoods of New York City to gain a greater understanding and appreciation of Puerto Rican culture. I also had the good fortune of spending time in foreign countries, where because either of my race or language I was clearly known as an outsider. These experiences of nondominant status created certain feelings and dynamics of relationships unbeknownst to me. Though difficult, these experiences have been enriching, as they help me to empathize with the "outsider" status of many underrepresented clients.

DEVELOPMENT OF GOALS

Regardless of theoretical orientation, the establishment of goals is essential for effective counseling to take place. Goals answer important questions such as: Why has the client come to counseling? What does the client want from counseling? When should counseling be terminated? Without goals, counseling will founder and lead to frustration. Goals help the counselor to establish leverage (Egan, 1998).

The concept of leverage is sometimes misunderstood—as it is interpreted to mean that the counselor has some kind of power, authority, or control over the client. The model put forth in this book is that counseling is a collaborative endeavor between counselor and client, and the establishment of goals and commitment to their attainment must also be mutual. In a first session, the counselor should ascertain two things: The first is what has brought the client to counseling; the second, how does the client imagine that counseling can help him or her? The latter question serves to disabuse the client of false notions of counseling, inform the client as to how the counselor intends to work, and allows the counselor to commit (or not commit) to the relationship based on what the client wants and the counselor's comfort and preparedness in dealing with such issues. When asked how counseling can help them, clients can give responses that the counselor is unable to accommodate. In my practice, responses have included: "I want some pills" or "I would like some help in killing myself." Other responses may go beyond the counselor's qualifications. For example, it would be difficult to treat someone who came for help with an eating disorder without any special knowledge or training.

The best the counselor could do would be to refer this client to someone who is trained to do such work. Leverage arises from this mutually agreed upon endeavor, from a clear idea on the part of both the counselor and the client as to why the client is in counseling and what he or she wishes to achieve. If counselors feel lost and the process is floundering with a client, it may well be because they have failed to establish leverage.

Goals Versus Wants

The establishment of goals may sound like an easy task; however, it is not. A requirement for establishing goals is knowing what one wants. How many of us, when asked, "What are your goals?" freeze up and feel put on the spot. Clients will feel the same way. Many times, supervisees will report that they asked clients for their goals and clients were unable to generate any. Anxious people will typically become more anxious when asked for their goals. Egan (1998) suggests that, rather than asking the client for goals, the counselor ask first for wants: What is it you really want? Discovering our truest and deepest wants is perhaps one of the greatest gifts life can offer; however, their discovery can be equally difficult. Therefore, the counselor must employ certain techniques to stimulate the client's thinking and feeling more creatively about his or her problem situation. A favorite is: "If you could wave a magic wand, how would things (or life or this problem) be different for you?" Questions such as this should generate a list of responses similar to what Egan (1998) calls "brainstorming." With this list, the counselor and client can work collaboratively in selecting responses that are realistic and will make a difference in the life of the client. This becomes the basis for goal setting.

If the development of the working alliance is geared toward answering the question, "Where is this client at the present moment and where has he or she come from?" Then the development of goals is geared toward answering the question, "Where does the client want to go?" This process is not necessarily linear but can be intertwined. In developing the working alliance, the counselor can be engaged in discovering with clients where they wish to go, and the reverse is also true. The third leg of the counseling process is described by Egan (1998) as strategy development and implementation. After discovering where one wants to go, the next question is: "How does one wish to get there?"

DEVELOPMENT OF STRATEGIES

Greater than the sadness of not knowing what one wants in life is perhaps knowing what one wants and not knowing how to achieve it. If counseling stopped at the discovery of wants or the making of goals, there would be a sad incompleteness about the whole process. In more traditional nomenclature, wants are converted into goals and the means for achieving them converted into objectives. However, some objectives can become subgoals, which in turn need their own objectives. For example, a depressed client wants to feel less depressed (goal) and feels that getting a job she likes (objective) would contribute to that goal. However, getting a job (subgoal) requires preparing a resume, reading the classifieds, going to an employment agency, and so forth (objectives). If necessary, preparing a resume can become a sub-subgoal with going to a library, getting a knowledgeable acquaintance to help, and so forth as objectives. This paradigm of goals and objectives helps to establish further leverage and build accountability into the counseling relationship. For example, if the client agreed that the coming week would be dedicated to going to the library for help with resume preparation, the counselor can follow up the next week by processing the experience or the resistance if the objective was not met.

This simplification of the individual counseling process does not mean to suggest that counseling proceeds in a neat, linear fashion. Having been trained psychodynamically, I have a strong appreciation and respect for the subtleties of counseling that can make it a gut-wrenching process. Nevertheless, in the age of managed care and the emphasis upon accountability and short-term treatment, working with goals and objectives is unavoidable. Most counseling agencies, whether hospital-based or community-based and regardless of theoretical orientation, utilize treatment plans organized around goals and objectives. These plans are reviewed and updated periodically according to the attainment or lack thereof of goals and objectives.

TRANSFERENCE AND COUNTERTRANSFERENCE

After a defense of working with goals and objectives, it might seem odd to include a section about transference and countertransference, typically associated with longer-term psychodynamic forms of counseling. Indeed, a bona fide interpersonal analyst would believe that much, if not all, of counseling is about the analysis of transference and countertransference. However, one need not be an analyst to appreciate that in an interpersonal encounter such as that between counselor and counselee, emotional reactions to each other will be frequent and even intense. These reactions, if given attention and processed, can contribute positively to counseling. If left unheeded, their contribution will be deleterious.

Transference

Not all the client's reactions toward the counselor should be classified as transference. "Transference is a manifestation of some of what a client has learned about human relationships in contacts with significant figures (e.g., mother, father, and siblings) during his or her formative years" (Gelso & Carter, 1994; Singer, 1965, as cited in Multon, Patton, & Kivilighan, 1996, p. 243). Behind this definition of transference is the assumption that the client will play out ("transfer") to the counselor significant issues regarding interpersonal relationships. If the counselor pays attention to such transfer, to how the client is relating, valuable information can be gleaned from the encounter. For client reactions to be labeled transferential in the traditional sense, they should meet the criteria of being intense, inappropriate, tenacious (they persist in spite of changes in the counselor's behavior), capricious, and ambivalent (Multon, Patton, & Kivilighan, 1996). These reactions can be positive (loving, sexual, erotic, indulgent) or negative (hostile, aggressive, angry, etc.). Freud (1912/1958) wrote:

> In every analytic treatment there arises an intense emotional relationship between the patient and the analyst. It can be of a positive or negative character and can vary between the extremes of a passionate, completely sensual love and the unbridled expression of an embittered defiance and hatred. (p. 102)

If counselors properly recognize transferential reactions, they will neither personalize them nor be frightened or overwhelmed by them, but will utilize them in benefit of the counseling process. However, not only reactions that can be traditionally classified as transferential can be used in this positive fashion; also useful are those reactions by the client that do not fit the classic criteria for transference. Positive and/or negative feelings toward the counselor or the counseling, perhaps not as intense or inappropriate, should also be given credence, processed, and used as "grist for the mill." A counselor must remember that a client can communicate such feelings in ways other than verbal, such as arriving very late or very early for appointments, not showing up at all or asking for more sessions, and, of course, through body language.

Unique to the counseling/psychotherapy profession is its respect for the emotional dimension of human existence. The individual counseling dyad can be seen as a training ground and laboratory for helping clients to deal appropriately with that dimension and its expression.

Countertransference

The renowned Harvard child psychiatrist Robert Coles once quipped how easy it was to go to a library and find volumes written about transference and how difficult to find even one book about countertransference. The implication is that counselors appear much more astute at understanding the acted-out, mangled parts of their clients, but much less so in understanding their own. Emotional reactions to clients are a necessary part of counseling, and how much credence they are given will depend on one's theoretical orientation. From an interpersonalist perspective, these reactions are important and can be either countertransferentially damaging or therapeutically facilitative.

Traditionally speaking, countertransferential reactions will meet the same criteria listed above for transferential reactions. No counselor is exempt from the possibility that clients, because of who they are, what they look like, or the nature of their problems, will tap into the counselor's unresolved and vulnerable issues. Countertransference, if left undetected or unmanaged, can result in great harm to clients as counselors transfer onto clients the nonintegrated parts of themselves.

However, there are counselor reactions that are not countertransferential and can be used in favor of the therapeutic process. These reactions are less about the counselor and more about the client and may be a reflection of how others see the client (Fontaine & Hammond, 1994). For example, such counselor reactions as feeling seduced, manipulated, angered, or afraid may be an indication of the intrapsychic make-up and interpersonal style of the client. A good counselor is able to monitor these reactions and utilize them in helping clients gain greater knowledge of themselves. The seasoned counselor learns to share reactions with the client in an appropriate and nonthreatening manner.

More than once, supervisees have asked: "How do I know the difference between a countertransferential and a noncountertransferential reaction?" This is an extremely important question because it can be reframed as: "How do I know whether my reaction is more about me or about my client?" Again, the criteria (intense, inappropriate, tenacious, capricious, and ambivalent) previously cited for transferential reactions are helpful, but some counselor reactions are more subtle than these criteria. The most valid answer to this question is: The greater the counselor's self-knowledge, the greater the capacity for distinguishing the two types of reactions. Thus, good supervision and the counselor's own counseling are two of the best ways to increase self-knowledge. In the end, it is a lifelong struggle, but one that makes the job interesting, exciting, and challenging. In any intense interpersonal encounter, both parties—with all their intrapsychic and cultural baggage—are emotionally penetrating one another. The counselor should always be aware there are two subjectivities involved in the counseling relationship. Moreover, when notions of culture, race, and ethnicity are introduced into the counseling relationship, the intersubjective penetration between counselor and client becomes even more intriguing, challenging, and potentially rewarding.

Transference and Countertransference in the Cross-Cultural Relationship

The concepts of transference and countertransference can be utilized in multicultural counseling. They serve to frame strong and irrational reactions by both the client and the counselor in terms of cultural conflict and cultural identity development.

In order for the concept of transference to be useful, one must go beyond the traditional analytical framework of the counselor as representative of the primary caretaker to the counselor as representative of a culture. Depending on clients' form of second-culture acquisition and level of cultural identity development, they will play out issues significant to cultural differences. For example, minority clients at the conformity stage easily will idealize a counselor from the dominant culture. From a multicultural perspective, it would be wrong to interpret such idealization as having to do with childhood dependency issues. Rather, it is more a function of how these minority clients see themselves in relation to the dominant culture. In a similar vein, a minority client at the resistance stage will transfer anger and depreciation to a counselor from the dominant culture, now seen as an instrument of oppression. Again, within the multicultural perspective, such transference should not be seen as stemming from conflicts with primary caretakers but as the result of this minority client's stage of development and how the client sees himself or herself in relation to the dominant culture. In short, when working with clients from nondominant cultures, transference issues based on race, ethnicity, sexual orientation, or gender will have more to do with the client's level of cultural identity development than with primary caretakers.

Much of what was said about transference in cross-cultural counseling can be said about countertransference. When working with clients from nondominant cultures, counselor's reactions will have more to do with their own level of cultural identity development. Counselors by nature are not exempt from racial/ethnic stereotypes. Thus, when working with nondominant clients who look, behave, and speak differently, counselors must be acutely honest in detecting whether their negative reactions to clients are the result of cultural imperialism. Obviously, the more highly developed a counselor's cultural identity, the greater the capacity for openness to and enrichment by clients from diverse cultures. An autonomous White counselor should have fewer countertransferential reactions to non-White clients. However, the same cannot be said for a disintegrated or reintegrated White counselor. Earlier mention was made of racial identity relationship types between counselor and client as being either progressive, regressive, parallel, or crossed. Crossed (counselor and client have directly opposite attitudes) and regressive (counselor is at a lower level of cultural identity development) relationships are most prone to countertransferential reactions. What was said in the first part of this chapter about the importance and difficulty of distinguishing countertransference from counselor reactions that reveal something accurate about the client must be reiterated here. Multicultural counselors should be courageously honest with themselves and their supervisors in admitting racist/sexist attitudes and ethnic/gender stereotypes that might result in negative reactions to culturally diverse clients. If it's mentionable, it's manageable. Much easier than the recognition of these mangled parts of ourselves is pathologizing the client. The sensitive multicultural counselor constantly will scrutinize how two diverse cultures (that of the counselor and that of the client) are impacting the counseling relationship and will be sensitive to counseling as a coinvestigation into reality.

CASE EXAMPLE

Identifying and Background Information

Tony is a 27-year-old, single, Puerto Rican male who is currently unemployed. The clinic director assigned Tony to me after he requested a change of counselors. Tony's chart revealed a long counseling/psychiatric history dating back to age eight, while he was still living in Puerto Rico. Over the years, he had been seen by several different counselors in the clinic, and treatment usually ended because of Tony's frequent returns to Puerto Rico. The latest intake/assessment revealed symptoms of anxiety and depression, for which he was receiving medication. Tony had stopped attending school after the ninth grade and had very little job history. From the chart, he appeared to be in good health except for occasional asthma. He was currently living with his mother and was never married.

After perusing the chart, I had ambivalent feelings about working with Tony. He had a long history of mental health involvement and was neither working nor going to school—which led me to feel that there would be little that could be accomplished with Tony besides case management. Yet there was something about this client that intrigued me. That he had requested another counselor piqued my curiosity and inspired me to succeed where others had failed.

Early Phase of Counseling

Tony failed to keep three appointments, about which I had notified him through the mail. The clinic's policy was that, after three consecutive broken appointments, the clinician was no longer obligated to schedule further meetings. If there was no contact for 90 days, the case would be closed automatically. I resigned myself to the idea that Tony and I would not be working together.

My memory is vague as to how Tony and I finally did meet. Perhaps it was the attending psychiatrist who urged him to continue counseling. In any event, Tony and I finally did have a first session. He explained the missed appointments as my having sent the letters to his mother's house, where he was no longer staying. Tony appeared about 6 feet tall, 170 pounds, and well-built, with long red hair and a freckled face. Because his English was very poor, all our counseling sessions were conducted in Spanish. During the first session, Tony was quite evasive and distant, making very little eye contact. I clearly felt he was checking me out. His most significant comments were about a previous female Hispanic counselor he had at the clinic and with whom he had looked forward to reconnecting upon his return from Puerto Rico. However, she had left the clinic, leaving Tony feeling quite distraught. He also had negative things to say about the counselor from whom he requested a transfer. Initially, it seemed to me that Tony was very identified with Puerto Rican culture. I was the first non-Hispanic counselor Tony had seen, and I knew this caused him some difficulty. Yet, the fact that I spoke Spanish fluently and self-assessed at the immersion-emersion stage of White racial identity development probably helped Tony not to dismiss me outright. I considered Tony at the dissonance stage, yet bordering on the resistance stage, of cultural identity development. As a result, I realized I had a progressive relationship with Tony and that this would help toward establishing a working alliance. In terms of the second-culture acquisition process, I felt Tony's mode of adaptation was basically one of rejection. His frequent returns to Puerto Rico, his warm and positive reflections on life in *la isla del encanto*, his relational life composed almost exclusively of Puerto Ricans, and his lack of English led me to believe that he had a very low identification with the dominant culture. I knew this would complicate matters between Tony and myself (a non–Puerto Rican), but I tried to maintain a position of openness, support, and genuine concern.

Three issues marked the early phase of counseling between Tony and myself: first, his grieving the loss of his counselor before he left for Puerto Rico; second, his potentially getting social security disability benefits; and third, his desire to learn hair styling. I gave Tony ample space to grieve the loss of Erica (his former counselor), and I connected him with a vocational center that catered especially to people with a mental health history. Regarding the facilitation of social security disability for Tony, I was truly conflicted. He was still young, and I was not totally convinced that his psychiatric history earned him the label of "disabled." Would promoting such be a form of disempowerment? On the other hand, Tony could have used the extra money (he was on welfare at the time), and he had previously tried unsuccessfully several times to get disability. When we began working together, Tony's new application was already in the works. This, together with the fact that he seemed motivated to take up a vocation, led me to support his claim for disability.

For some unknown reason, Tony's disability claim was accepted this time after several failed attempts. How much this contributed to solidifying the working relationship with Tony, I don't know. Though we got off to a rocky start (Tony continued to miss appointments but less frequently, and he would call to cancel if he was unable to attend), we had managed to develop a mutual liking and respect. I took a great deal of interest in Tony's world, culturally different from my own, and I think he sensed this interest. However, little did I know that I would learn things about Tony that would make our worlds even more culturally diverse.

Middle Phases of Counseling

After several weeks of counseling, Tony began sharing with me his social/relational world. Tony had a homosexual partner of several years, a relationship that he described as very satisfying. This admission caused me no great consternation; I had given time and effort to working through my homophobia and felt in touch with my own homoerotic parts. Thus, I felt that my sexual identity was developed enough to open myself to the gay world of my client. However, I did realize that Tony was now assuming a double minority status—being both gay and Hispanic. In terms of his gay/minority identity development, Tony evidenced no conflict being gay, had homosexual and heterosexual friends of both genders, and appeared relatively unconcerned about my sexual orientation—unlike my ethnicity. I considered Tony to be at the integrative awareness stage of identity development vis-à-vis his homosexuality and considered us to have a parallel relationship regarding issues of sexual identity. However, I was less prepared for what Tony would share next.

Tony also revealed that he was *una draga*. He used this Spanish term, and I was unfamiliar with it. After some clarification, I came to understand that *una draga* was the Spanish translation of "drag queen"—and drag queens belong to a world with which I was totally unfamiliar. I wanted very much to explore this world with Tony, but it was difficult for me to discern whether this desire was for Tony's benefit or some kind of voyeurism on my part. Tony explained how much he enjoyed dressing up as a woman and going out, but he also admitted that this sometimes caused problems with his partner. Tony insisted that he did not work as a prostitute nor did he have any sex except with this partner. A crucial moment in the counseling process came when Tony explained that in his other world he was really "Tanya" and not Tony. I asked him at one point if he wanted me to call him Tanya, and he said it didn't matter but if I wanted to it was okay. I took this to mean yes, and I began transitioning from Tony to Tanya, which in Spanish has implications in addition to just the names. I also now had to use the feminine forms of agreement when speaking to Tanya. I made mistakes but after a while became more comfortable. Tanya also shared that she was beginning hormonal treatments to develop her breasts. When I asked about a genital operation, she was not sure. Tanya was taking me places I had never been before. She allowed me to enter her world, one that I both judged and respected. It never occurred to me at the time to label Tanya with gender identity disorder. I was very concerned about her sexual activity, but she reassured me of her monogamy. I found myself wondering more often than I wanted how Tanya looked and what she did dressed as a woman. Tanya evidenced a great deal of self-acceptance concerning who she was and made it clear that changing that dimension of her life in no way should be the goal of counseling. She continued at the vocational center but had complaints about her coworkers, whom she experienced as judgmental. It was hard not to be judgmental of Tanya. Her triple minority status (Hispanic, gay, transvestite/transsexual) pushed the limits of cultural sensitivity. I had to admit that I was less open to Tanya's drag queen world and probably was in a regressive relationship vis-à-vis my world of a beer with the boys after work, yet I was careful not to jeopardize the strong relationship we had established. I remember telling Tanya I would miss one week (she came quite regularly now). When she inquired as to why, I told her I was going on a ski trip, and she appeared concerned. When I asked about her concern, she remarked that perhaps I would meet a nice woman, get married, and not return to counseling. Without delving into the transferential issues, I took Tanya's comment to be an indication of the strong bond we had developed despite our many cultural differences. She would miss me, and that made me feel good.

Nevertheless, Tanya's anxiety continued, and she was still taking medication. This both perturbed and mystified me. Tanya seemed so at ease with many aspects of her life that something was missing to explain her anxiety and difficulty with being with groups of people.

Final Phases of Counseling

A breakthrough came with a revelation that was very difficult for Tanya. She prepared me by saying she was afraid to mention it and wondered desperately what I might say or do. After my processing these feelings for some time and using all my skill at breaking through resistance, Tanya finally told me she had had a severe addiction to marijuana for many years. Her addiction was such that, upon waking in the morning, the first thing she did was smoke a joint. Internally, I reacted strongly. I have a great deal of countertransference toward addicts, and I knew I would be tested entering Tanya's world of addiction. Here was another counselee (I had dealt with many) receiving mental health services when the real problem was drug addiction and the real solution drug rehabilitation. I assumed that Tanya mentioned it because she wanted help. Therefore, I took a strong stand and said she must go to rehab if we were to continue counseling. Fortunately, a drug rehab program was housed in the clinic; I facilitated the referral. Tanya was reluctant, saying she didn't want to be in any groups, knowing that many drug rehab programs required such participation. I refused to back down, insisted she must go, and told her that I would continue to see her only under those conditions. I realized I could lose the relationship with Tanya, but I thought the risk was worth it. The rehab program started Tanya on intense acupuncture treatment, and the results were almost miraculous. Tanya came to counseling overjoyed at how much the treatment was helping her. She had even started attending a group. Tanya had given me permission to speak with the person in charge of her rehab, and they too were impressed with her progress.

I left the clinic for a new job, which brought our relationship to an end. Tanya's marijuana addiction seemed to be under control; consequentially, her anxiety and paranoia were considerably reduced. She continued training as a hairstylist, but the director of the vocational center was less impressed with Tanya's progress because he felt Tanya really didn't want a job. Had I continued counseling with Tanya, I would have negotiated more seriously with her, making a job and a career the primary goals of counseling.

SUMMARY

I have fond memories of my relationship with Tanya. Patience with and openness to someone culturally very different than myself allowed Tanya to develop the necessary trust that resulted in the admission of her marijuana addiction. It was an important revelation because I do believe it was the primary cause of her emotional symptoms. Issues of acculturation and cultural identity development exist along various dimensions in this case: race, ethnicity, and sexual orientation and identity. Tanya was a member of several nondominant cultures that underlay her sensitivity and vulnerability. At first, I hypothesized that such marginality was overly stressful and resulted in symptoms of anxiety and depression, but there was more to

Tanya's story. The culture of addiction had a primary place in her life. Eliminating her use of marijuana allowed Tanya to sustain her nondominant identities without the emotional symptoms that had plagued her for so very long.

REFERENCES

Cormier, W.H., & Cormier, L.S. (1990). *Interviewing strategies for helpers: Fundamental skills and cognitive behavioral interventions.* Pacific Grove, CA: Brooks/Cole.

Doyle, R.E. (1992). *Essential skills and strategies in the helping process.* Pacific Grove, CA: Brooks/Cole.

Duan, C., & Hill, C.E. (1996). The current state of empathy research. *Journal of Counseling Psychology, 43,* 261–274.

Egan, G.E. (1998). *The skilled helper: A problem management approach to helping.* Pacific Grove, CA: Brooks/Cole.

Fontaine, J.H., & Hammond, N.L. (1994) Twenty counseling maxims. *Journal of Counseling and Development, 73,* 223–226.

Freud, S. (1958). The dynamics of transference. In J. Strachey (Ed. and Trans.), *The standard edition of the complete psychological works of Sigmund Freud* (Vol. 12, pp. 97–108) London: Hogarth Press. (Original work published 1912)

Gelso, C.J., & Carter, J.A. (1994). Components of the psychotherapy relationship: Their interactions and unfolding during treatment. *Journal of Counseling Psychology, 41,* 296–306 .

Ivey, A.E. (1995). Psychotherapy as liberation: Toward specific skills and strategies in multicultural counseling and therapy. In J. G. Ponterotto, J.M. Casas, L.A. Suzuki, & C.M. Alexander (Eds.), *Handbook of multicultural counseling* (pp. 53–72). Thousand Oaks, CA: Sage.

Meier, S.T., & Davis, S.R. (1997). *The elements of counseling.* Pacific Grove, CA: Brooks/Cole.

Multon, K.D., Patton, M.J., & Kivilighan, D.M. (1996). Development of the Missouri Identifying Transference Scale. *Journal of Counseling Psychology, 43,* 243–252.

Rogers, C.R. (1959). A theory of therapy, personality and interpersonal relationships as developed in the client-centered framework. In S. Koch (Ed.), *Psychology: A study of a science. Study 1. Conceptual and systematic: Vol. 3. Formulations of the person and the social context* (pp. 184–256). New York: McGraw-Hill.

—《v/v》—

MULTICULTURAL GROUP COUNSELING

The literature on multicultural group counseling is scant, which raises some immediate questions. If what defines the human is the interpersonal/ social dimension and groups provide an ideal setting for examining and growing in our interpersonal dimension, why does there seem to be such resistance to forming groups with diverse clients? The assumption behind this chapter is that groups composed of members from diverse cultural backgrounds are excellent laboratories for grappling with issues of diversity and can generate significant positive consequences in the larger society. However, before the potential richness of multicultural group counseling can be explored, it is necessary to examine the difficulty in and resistance to forming groups—on the part of both the counselor and the client.

RESISTANCE TO GROUPS

The most fundamental principle of group counseling is: *Groups create anxiety*. How many of us when told at a workshop or similar event, "You will now be broken up into groups," experience a rush of adrenalin?

Almost immediately, anxiety-provoking questions arise in our minds, questions such as: What will my group be like? Who will be in my group? Will they like me? Will I like them? Will anybody I know be in my group? Will I be asked to do or say something that makes me uncomfortable? These and questions like them are not uncommon and, when applied to ongoing counseling groups, provoke even more anxiety. Most clinicians feel more comfortable in a dyadic relationship. If the counselor wishing to start a group is a novice in group work, the not-so-conscious resistance can be quite strong. The management of transference in a group is much more challenging than that of the individual counseling relationship (Shields & Lanza, 1993). Just as does the client, the counselor risks being exposed to an entire group, as opposed to a single individual. Making a "mistake" before an individual client is less invasive than making one before an entire group.

I worked for a long period of time in a clinic where the entire staff agreed over and over again that more group counseling was both clinically and economically indicated. However, very few groups ever materialized. Staff were quick to place most of the blame on client resistance, reporting that their clients did not feel comfortable talking about their problems in front of others. No doubt there was client resistance, but the staff colluded in that resistance. If the counselor is ambivalent toward the formation of a group, it removes the possibility of working through client resistance. Moreover, some clients may feel betrayed being asked by their counselors to relinquish (or share) the intimacy of the individual counseling environment for that of a group (Shields & Lanza, 1993).

Another aspect of resistance to group formation arises when a counselor in an agency setting is recruiting group members via other staff. Colleagues may be unwilling to share their individual clients to a group working with another clinician. The site of my predoctoral internship had as a requirement that every intern lead a group. However, due to the number of interns that year, there were not enough existing groups for interns to lead. The group supervisor asked that I, being Spanish-speaking, begin my own group by recruiting Spanish-speaking clients from clinicians who only spoke English. The idea seemed quite plausible to supervisors who were anxious to provide more Spanish-speaking services in the agency. However, the result was disappointing and very few referrals were made. Months later, in a process session with the staff, several admitted to not wanting to "share" their clients, fearing that they would be upstaged (by an intern no less!) and their clients would enjoy the Spanish-speaking service to the extent of not wanting to be in individual counseling. Competition (so prevalent in groups and to be explored later) seemed to ignite a parallel process among the staff. Counselors may feel anxious having their clients exposed to another clinician (Shields & Lanza, 1993).

Groups are difficult to form—not only for the dynamic reasons just presented but also for simple logistical reasons, such as finding an agreeable time and day for members to meet. When one adds the challenge posed by diversity, only a clinician who is overwhelmingly convinced of the therapeutic value of groups will persevere in starting and sustaining them. It is hoped that the fundamentals of group counseling presented in this chapter will add to that conviction.

FUNDAMENTALS OF GROUP COUNSELING

The attempt here is to present some of the more general constructs in group counseling. It is not meant to be exhaustive nor free of the author's own theoretical biases, but intends to give the reader a dynamic overview of group functioning and its potentially rich healing power.

The Group as Social Microcosm

The social microcosm metaphor reveals that a group of people, given sufficient time and a minimal amount of structure, will begin to manifest behaviors typical of their interpersonal functioning in the larger outside world (Yalom, 1995). The group "becomes a miniaturized representation of each patient's social universe" (Yalom 1995, p. 42). The therapeutic difference and power of the group is that a member's interpersonal behaviors and style can be scrutinized primarily through feedback from other group members. Thus, connected to the social microcosm metaphor is another: the group as a laboratory for interpersonal learning and development (Egan, 1973). As a scientist uses a microscope to examine particles and understand their relationship to the whole, so too is the group a microscope for examining parts of an individual's behavior in relationship to a wider context, that of the group and the outside world.

More importantly, the learning that takes place in group is *experiential* (Johnson & Johnson, 1994). If the group is able to function at a high level, members will actively participate, risking examination by self and others of their interpersonal idiosyncrasies and maladaptive behaviors. One learns by doing, which results in knowledge gained through how one experiences other members of the group and how one is experienced by the other members. Greater insight and awareness into oneself are gained through actual interaction among group members. Yalom (1995) talks about the reflective loop necessary for learning in groups. There occurs an experience in group (most likely a significant interaction between oneself and another member or members), reflection upon the experience, cognitive insight into the experience, and a return to further interaction. Too often counseling revolves around the more cognitive, insight-oriented aspects of self-awareness but does not provide the affective experience that must accompany such insight for real change to take place. Yalom (1995) talks about the corrective experience in groups as having two dimensions: one must *experience* something strongly and one must *understand* the implications of that experience.

Groups, more likely than individual counseling, will provide these strong emotional experiences. Given sufficient time and space, members will experience each other with strong emotions. The key is to use such emotional reactions as a wonderful opportunity for gaining greater understanding of oneself. The following is a more in-depth look at some possible reasons why groups are charged with so much emotional power.

The Group as Mother

Earlier, reference was made to the numerous anxiety-provoking questions that arise when an individual is faced with the prospect of being part of a group. Bion (1961), in his classic essay, *Experience in Groups*, explains this anxiety or tension as the result of bipolar feelings between the unconscious fear of being fused with the group to the extent of losing one's identity and the fear of being a person in isolation, totally separated from the group. Wells (1990), drawing upon object-relations theorists such as

Klein and Mahler, relates this struggle to that of the infant who seeks at the same time to be both one with and separated from Mother. The chapter on second-culture acquisition made reference to the developing infant as experiencing a mother who is both good and bad, both nurturing and frustrating—resulting in ambivalent feelings of love and hate. Groups, such as mothers, "create strong, conflicting ambivalent feelings of love and hate...groups both nurture and scold...groups are needed yet resented...groups create feelings of bliss and despair" (Wells, 1990, p. 59). Bion (1961) referred to individuals as group animals at war with themselves—drawn by their very nature to group involvement while at the same time fighting against their "groupishness."

Obviously, how this tension and anxiety resolves itself with and among group members is the meat and potatoes of group work. At the beginning, the threat of isolation is far stronger than that of fusion. The first defense against this primal anxiety is the denial of differences and the search for commonalities. When beginning a class on group counseling, I have students break up into dyads and participate in a "get-to-know-the-other-person" exercise. They take turns talking about themselves and then come back to the larger group and inform them what they learned about their partner. During these reports, members constantly intersperse phrases such as: "she's just like me...," "we've had the same experience...," "it's like we've known each other...," and other such phrases indicating strong similarity with the other member. Just as does the infant who in the early stages of development seeks a symbiotic relationship with Mother to calm the terrors of anxiety about strangers, members in the early life of a group seek oneness with the group (Alonso & Rutan, 1984).

During this beginning time of the group, the symbiosis among the members, the consequence of primal fear over being alone, results in very little, if any, significant client revelation as members feel very little of their individuality (Alonso & Rutan, 1984). This stage of group life is very dependent upon the leader, who is perceived as the good parent, a source of protection and nourishment. Obviously, this form of regressed existence does not endure forever. It does not take long for "sibling rivalries," competition, sexual tensions, struggles for dominance and status, or differences in background and values to emerge (Yalom, 1995). These cause multiple transferences to take place among members, including the leader. In groups, these transferences are managed by a common defense mechanism known as projective identification, a concept examined more closely in the following section.

Projective Identification

Problems associated with interpersonal life result from our frequent inability to see others as they are in favor of seeing them as how we need them to be to satisfy our own intrapsychic needs. Famed theorists have used different concepts to refer to this universal dynamic: Freud (1958) called it transference; Sullivan (1953), "parataxic distortion"; and Klein (1946), "projective identification." Though there are differences in how these terms are used, they can be regarded as having a common thread, which is the reference to the "distortion of *inter*personal reality in response to *intra*personal needs" (Yalom, 1995, p. 20; italics added). The elaboration of projective identification is consistent with the metaphor of group as Mother and an object relations perspective.

Consistent reference has been made to the developing infant's ambivalent experience of Mother. The experience as both nourishing and frustrating generates conflictual feelings of love and hate toward the same figure. This ambivalence is not sustainable and results in *splitting*, "a primitive psychological mechanism used where an individual disowns parts of self that are undesirable" (Wells, 1990, p. 58). In the case of the infant, hate feelings need to be disowned and therefore are split off. However, something needs to be done with these disowned parts of ourselves, and this is accomplished through the mechanism of projective identification, "a psychological mechanism by which individuals unconsciously identify with an object (person, event, attitude) by externalizing (projecting) split (disowned) parts of themselves" (Wells, 1990, p. 68). The infant typically projects the split-off hate feelings onto Daddy, with the result that Mommy is all good and Daddy is all bad; Mommy loves me, and Daddy hates me. Both are distortions, but children's intrapsychic demands are satisfied as they no longer have to tolerate love/hate feelings toward the same person. In this case, the object (Father) is seen as having acquired the disowned characteristics (hateful feelings) of the self (the infant), and the result is: "I don't hate Mommy; Daddy hates me." In groups, the disowned parts of ourselves are easily projected onto other members, and this becomes the fundamental principle behind role differentiation in groups. "Each group member can become a receptacle for the projected parts of their cohorts" (Wells, 1990, p. 64).

However, before examining more closely the development of group roles, it is necessary to clarify that the disowned parts of oneself are not necessarily in themselves negative. For example, group members may split off their leadership dimension and project it onto another member or the group leader. If this happens en masse, the result is a very dependent group with all leadership embodied in one person. Cults and cult leaders are notorious for activating this type of dynamic, with the sometimes extreme result of mass suicide: The leader dies so I must also die. In these cases, there is a positive identification with the object of projection as opposed to when the disowned aspect of self is negative (i.e., something I don't like about myself), resulting in rejection (equaling negative identification) with the object of projection (Segal, 1964, as cited in Wells, 1990).

Development of Roles in Groups

Theorists widely recognize that group members given sufficient time and space will develop roles in the group. There is disagreement as to what exactly these roles are. Yalom (1995) lists the following: task leader, social-emotional leader, provocateur, doctor's helper, help-rejecting complainer, self-righteous moralist, "star," group hysteric, technical executive leader, social secretary, group stud, group critic, group romantic, guardian of democracy, timekeeper, aggressive male, vigilante of honesty, scrutinizer, innocent, scapegoat, intellectualizer, child, puritan, and reintegrator, along with the sociable role, the structural role, the divergent role, and the cautionary role. Rather than define these, a more important purpose is the understanding of how roles develop in group members. Naivete may lead us in the direction of thinking that a member's role in group is simply a result of intrapersonal makeup. However, common sense tells us this is not true, as people take on different roles in different social situations. The same person may be silent in one and talkative in another.

Role differentiation is the result of mutual projective identifications among group members. The more excessive the projective identification, the more rigid the role differentiation. Group members collude in splitting off a common undesirable aspect of themselves and imbue a certain member with that quality. The reader can take any one of the many roles listed above and explain its development through projection. For example, let's take the role of the scapegoat, since it is very prevalent and potentially quite damaging in group relations. In the Judaic-Christian tradition, the sacrificial lamb fulfilled the role of scapegoat. Imbued with the sins of the community, it was sacrificed (destroyed) and the community purified of its sinfulness. This purification needed to take place on a regular basis. The scapegoat in groups is the receptacle of all the projected bad (sinful?), weak, inadequate parts of the other members. In severe scapegoating, that particular member must be ostracized from the group. This happens many times in the world of work, where the failures of a work group are localized in one person who then needs to be dismissed for the work to go forward. Ironically, another arises to fulfill the same role, as the group finds it easier to have a scapegoat than to examine each member's weaknesses or parts of themselves that contributed to failure. "The search for a scapegoat or scapegoats typically begins after the group experiences aggression or frustration" (Wells, 1990, p. 72). The scenario goes like this: "I'm feeling inadequate" (inadequacy becomes a disowned part of self) results in "I'm fine" and "You're inadequate" (object of projection). Besides that of scapegoat, many other group roles can be explained by this complementary process of splitting and projection.

The question often arises as to why a certain member is chosen to fulfill a certain role by the group. There may not be an answer to this question other than the esoteric dynamics of group life. Sometimes, the collusion around projective identification is based upon physical appearance or something a group member might say. In this sense, members do, to a certain extent, audition for certain roles. However, in multicultural group counseling (which we will be discussing shortly), the projections are often around stereotypes based on race, ethnicity, gender, sexual orientation, and other similarly provocative dimensions of the human self. Once a projective identification has taken place, the subject(s) (group member or members doing the projecting) can behave in such a way as to evoke behaviors from the object of projection that conform to the subject's perceptions (Zinner, 1976). In the case of the scapegoat, the power of the group is such that the selected individual will behave in ways that appear inadequate to the rest of the group. Since certain groups need certain roles, counselors should never underestimate the power of projective identification. On the other hand, facilitating the group's awareness of this dynamic can be an equally powerful form of interpersonal learning.

The Establishment of Norms

An important dimension of group life is the construction of norms for how the group will function and behaviors that are acceptable and unacceptable. Norms are the result of members' expectations and directions from both the group leader and the more influential members of the group (Yalom, 1995). Norms can be both explicit and implicit. Examples of explicit norms are expectations about attendance, confidentiality, purpose of the group, and so forth. More important, though, are the implicit (unwritten) norms of the group resulting from specific behaviors—at first by the group leader and later by more influential members. Some examples of implicit norms are the group as agent of change, self-disclosure as a primary means for group development, acceptability of feedback from other members, respectful challenge/confrontation among members, and the group as a safe and supporting environment. None of these develop as the result of members being told how they should conduct themselves in the group. They develop only as the result of a common, implicit agreement among the members that the group will function according to such norms.

Group leaders should never underestimate the influence of their own behavior upon the development of group norms. Especially at the beginning, members tend to model their behavior upon that of the leader's. If the leader is quick to react, so too will be the members; if the leader is encouraging and supportive, so too will be the members; if the leader self-discloses appropriately, so too will the members. Norms should be related to the overall purpose of the group. If the group exists to foster interpersonal learning and growth, then the norms ought to promote such a goal. Therefore, the skilled group leader constantly will support and model behaviors that are consistent with the overall purpose of the group.

Stages of Groups

It is widely recognized that groups move through stages in the journey toward higher functioning and greater interpersonal learning (Jacobs, Harvill, & Masson, 1994; Wheelan, 1994; Yalom, 1995). Theorists will differ in the number of and nomenclature for these stages. The purpose here is to give the reader a simplified and generalized overview of group development.

Dependency Stage. The early life of a group is marked by dependency as members look to the leader for guidance and direction. There was an earlier explanation as to how entrance into a group has a regressive effect, with the delusion of being a perfectly happy family. The leader is perceived as all good, the perfect parent, and other members as being similar to oneself. Issues of acceptance and rejection are at the forefront, and for this reason the group functions at a very superficial level with the conversation being very polite and advice-giving the most common response to a member's problem or difficulty. No one wishes to rock the boat lest he or she be perceived as an inappropriate group member.

Conflict Stage. The "womblike" environment of the dependency stage changes radically as groups develop and issues of control and power replace those of belonging or not belonging. "Sibling rivalry" substitutes the "happy family" metaphor, and members jockey for position over and against other members. As a result, subgrouping is typical in this stage of development, along with hostility toward the leader—who has transitioned from being the good parent to a bad parent (Alonso & Rutan, 1984) by frustrating the dependency needs of the group. There is also "the gradual recognition by each member that one will not become the leader's favorite child" (Yalom, 1995, p. 298).

Work Stage. If the group has been able to negotiate the rough waters of the conflict stage, it will emerge trusting, cohesive (Wheelan, 1994), and ready to do the interpersonal work necessary for therapeutic change. Members engage in examination of their reactions and interactions with the group as a whole, and with individual members, and are willing to receive feedback from the group. In psychodynamic terms, it is the stage of group life marked by the analysis and understanding of the projective identifications on both an individual and group level as well as the consequential role one is playing in the group. It is both a painful and rewarding time for members—they experience the confrontation by the group around the unintegrated parts of themselves while at the same time reaping the fruits of greater self-knowledge.

Termination. Counseling groups eventually must end. Some are time-limited groups, and even ongoing groups do not have infinite life. Termination can cause members to regress (Wheelan, 1994) and act out their feelings around the ending of the relationship because, just as in individual counseling, it can evoke the memories of other terminated relationships. The skilled group counselor will be able to facilitate an expression of such feelings while at the same time allowing the group members to dwell on the fruits of their labor.

Groups do not necessarily pass through these stages in a neat, linear fashion, and some theorists have proposed many more stages. However, dependency, conflict, work, and termination are widely recognized, and the group counselor would do well to keep them as a framework for understanding the developmental life of groups. It is hoped that some of the metaphors used to articulate the fundamentals of group counseling in this chapter have given the reader an appreciation for the potential richness of group life. When one adds the multicultural dimension, that richness is magnified; but so too are the challenges. Following is an integration of multicultural aspects in group counseling.

MULTICULTURAL GROUP COUNSELING

Merta (1995) reminds the reader that one of the first applications of Kurt Lewin's T-groups was to reduce interracial tensions by working with community leaders back in the late 1940s and early 1950s. Thus, it is quite ironic to speak of a dearth of literature regarding multicultural group counseling when the intention of perhaps the greatest group theorist of this century, Lewin, was to apply his method of working to multicultural issues.

The increasing diversity of our society will make multiracial/ethnic groups more the rule than the exception. Current projections estimate that by the year 2030 there will be as many non-Whites as Whites living in the United States. If one of the components of effective group counseling is the creation of a social microcosm, culturally diverse counseling groups will be more reflective of today's reality. For this reason alone, the clinician is encouraged to form such groups, but their success will depend to a large extent upon the leader's facility in dealing with such diversity.

Heterogeneous Versus Homogeneous Groups

The decision to compose heterogeneous or homogeneous groups revolves around the debate that one is more productive than the other. On the one hand, there is the belief that group members who are similar will behave more cohesively and more productively; on the other hand, it is thought that members who are different will produce the greatest amount of change in each other. The problem framed as an either/or situation is overly simplistic, as heterogeneity and homogeneity should be seen in light of the group's purpose and along different dimensions. In other words, according to what variables should group members be seen as homogeneously or heterogeneously appropriate? Yalom (1995) recommends that leaders forming groups strive for heterogeneity in conflict areas and homogeneity in ego strength. Regardless of similarity among other variables, group members with a lot of disparity in their ability to handle conflict will find it extremely difficult to achieve cohesiveness.

Homogeneous Groups. The emphasis upon the importance of creating and running diverse counseling groups is not meant to eliminate a proper place for culturally homogeneous groups. Though no group can be completely homogenous, one can control the degree of homogeneity or heterogeneity (Johnson & Johnson, 1994). There are a number of examples in the literature dealing with racially homogenous groups for Asians (Chu & Sue, 1984; Ho, 1984; Lee, Juan, & Hom, 1984), for Hispanics (Acosta & Yamamoto, 1984; Comas-Diaz, 1984), for Blacks (Brown, 1984; Davis, 1984; McRoy & Oglesby, 1984), and for American Indians (Edwards & Edwards, 1984). Being with others in a similar situation or having the same goal can readily establish a feeling of connectedness, offer more immediate support, and keep conflicts to a minimum (Yalom, 1995). However, there are some disadvantages to homogeneous groups. According to Johnson and Johnson (1994), excessively homogeneous groups tend to be risk-avoidant, to lack in creative thinking and good decision making, to have difficulty adapting, and to frequently engage in groupthink. This last phenomenon refers to a group dynamic that discourages dissent and critical judgment (Janis, 1982).

Heterogeneous Groups. Heterogeneous groups operate from the assumption that differences among members can be used positively to promote a higher level of functioning among the members. In contrast to homogenous groups, initial anxiety in heterogeneous groups is extraordinarily high and thus the risk of premature termination is augmented. Skilled group leaders will recognize this and do their best initially to lessen the anxiety, perhaps through more structured work (Davis, 1984). Anxiety is a necessary part of group work, and how members deal with their anxiety becomes a therapeutic dimension of group work. However, too much anxiety, especially during the early life of a group, can be overwhelming to members—just as too little anxiety will stagnate the group. The challenge for every leader is the regulation of the level of anxiety in the group to achieve maximum therapeutic effectiveness. Though heterogeneous groups, at least at the beginning, are less cohesive and more conflictive, emerging empirical evidence indicates that heterogeneous groups (based on different levels and types of ability) are more effective on performance and decision-making tasks than are homogenous groups (Jackson, 1992).

Racially Heterogeneous Groups. Given the positives and negatives of heterogeneous groups, the formation of multiracial/multi-ethnic counseling groups should not be haphazard. For example, the inclusion of only one minority member in a group could very well lead to an intolerable degree of isolation for that member. Interestingly, if that minority member were at the preencounter or conformity stages of identity development, he or she might relish the idea of being in a group whose members were all from the majority culture. However, the probability that a group of this composition would promote the racial/cultural identity development of the minority member is very low. (Racial/cultural identity development in groups will be discussed in a later section.)

In general, racially diverse groups initially will provoke more anxiety than homogeneous groups. The anxiety will probably be greater for White members, as they may be less accustomed to being in intimate settings with racial/ethnic minorities. However, the opposite is not true: Minority members *are* accustomed to being in settings with a White majority (Davis, 1984; Greeley, Garcia, Kessler, & Gilchrest, 1992; Helms, 1990). Whites are typically reluctant to be in a group in which they are not the majority; they are simply not used to it. Regarding the composition between Blacks and Whites, empirical evidence suggests that Whites prefer groups that are 80% White and 20% Black, while Blacks are comfortable in groups that are 50% White and 50% Black (Davis, 1979). Currently, there is no research available to suggest that these proportions extend to other minority groups. Nevertheless, one is forced to speculate, for example, about how many women can men tolerate in a group; or how many homosexuals can heterosexuals tolerate. Counselors, when forming groups composed of members from majority and minority cultures, need to keep these questions in mind.

The amount and kind of heterogeneity will affect the level of the group's anxiety. The skilled group leader will create sufficient anxiety for therapeutic effectiveness but not too much to cause members to feel so uncomfortable that they drop out. This regulation of anxiety extends to considerations of group composition, as excessive heterogeneity along certain variables (e.g., ego strength) may be equally as unproductive as excessive homogeneity.

Projective Identification in Multicultural Groups

In groups composed of members from different racial, ethnic, and cultural backgrounds, the distortions, projections, and tranferences among members are likely to take the form of biases about and stereotypes of certain groups (Merta, 1995). In fact, projective identifications will be more immediate, as many of them will be based on physical appearance (skin color, gender, and so forth). For example, a male who stereotypes women as being all emotion with little capacity for reason will easily split off his emotions (because of some discomfort with them) and project them onto the women in the group, thus confirming his stereotypical view of women. Or a White person who views Blacks as inferior very easily will split off his own feelings of inferiority and project them onto the Black member(s) of the group, thereby providing evidence of his racist views. Or the heterosexual who stereotypes gays as being sexually inappropriate easily splits off his or her own homoerotic parts, projects them onto the gay member(s) of the group, and confirms for himself or herself that the gay member(s) is actively seeking sexual relations with him or her.

If the group leader is comfortable dealing with issues of gender, race, and sexual orientation, then the underlying dynamics of projective identification can be exposed. If the group is racially diverse, it would be appropriate for the group leader in the early stages to facilitate a discussion of the group's racial composition (Davis, 1984). The group most likely will resist dealing with candescent topics such as race, gender, and sexual orientation, but the group leader's comfort and facility with these issues will determine to a large extent the comfort level of the group. Even if the group resists, the counselor—by externalizing the issue—has communicated to the group that future discussion of such issues is permitted. Evidence suggests that groups intentionally led in discussing and exploring racial/cultural identity attitudes are more likely to modify such attitudes than groups where there is no exploration or where the exploration is haphazard (Burke, 1984; Davis, 1984; Helms, 1990; Merta, 1995). The counselor should always keep in mind a fundamental principle of human interaction: *If it's mentionable it's manageable and anything human is mentionable.* If conflictual issues in a group are not mentioned (and racial/cultural diversity is certainly one of them), they will be acted out in ways that are usually deleterious to group life. Thus, the counselor's own level of racial/cultural identity development will be crucial to the identity development of the group, as only a highly developed counselor will facilitate and allow such issues to be a productive part of group life.

Racial/Cultural Identity Development in Groups

Helms (1990) pointed out that, rather than race itself, the racial identity development stages of the group members are what determine the quality and effectiveness of a culturally diverse group. Along with looking at the number of majority versus minority members, one must examine how many members are at any particular stage of development. Obviously, the greater the number at any one stage of development, the more influential they will be in the life of the group (Helms, 1990). Furthermore, some stages of racial/cultural identity development are more influential because of the attitudes associated with that particular stage. For example, a subgroup of three Whites in the reintegration stage will be more influential than a subgroup of five or six contact Whites and more influential than a subgroup of one contact White, one disintegrated White, one reintegrated White, and one pseudoindependent White. Because of the attitude, affect, and cognition associated with the reintegration phase, a small number can influence greatly.

In the first part of this chapter, I discussed the establishment of norms as an important dimension of group life and how they result from more influential members. In multicultural groups, one must think more in terms of majority versus minority when it comes to the establishment of norms. If a counseling group is indeed a social microcosm, then reflected in the group will be the more influential majority and less influential minority of the larger society. For example, the fact that Whites have more status than non-Whites in the United States will play itself out in the group. Other variables, as mentioned above, such as the number of Whites and non-Whites in the group along with their stages of racial identity development will affect the level of influence. One must also consider that some members will have double or even triple minority status (Helms, 1990) based on race, gender, and level of racial identity development. For example, a White woman at the autonomy stage in a group dominated by men at lower levels of racial identity development would have double minority status. First, as a woman and secondly as representing an attitude toward non-Whites in contrast to the majority. If this particular woman were a lesbian, she would achieve triple minority status. Thus, racial identity development of group members is to be considered a variable that can affect one's status in the group.

Furthermore, in multicultural groups racial/cultural identity development levels can be responsible for subgroupings and coalitions (Helms,

1990). As mentioned in the first part of this chapter, coalitions and sub-groups are one way members deal with their anxiety and fear of being isolated and alone in the group. In multicultural groups, coalitions will tend to form around those sharing the same or near the same racial/cultural identity development level. More interestingly, coalitions can also form across racial/cultural lines, provided that such relationships are complementary. For example, Whites at lower levels of racial identity development—contact, disintegration, and even reintegration (provided it is not an active reintegration)—may welcome non-Whites at the preencounter or conformity stage. Since the conformity stage is marked by a desire to take on the identity of the majority culture, non-Whites also may cherish the opportunity to be part of such a coalition. Coalitions themselves will enjoy either majority or minority status (Helms, 1990). For example, a coalition of White's and non-Whites formed around the autonomy and integrative awareness stages may be a minority and less influential than a coalition formed around the contact and conformity stages, since the latter are more representative of the views of larger society.

Needless to say, the role of the leader in facilitating the development of racial identity within a group setting is crucial. Knowledge of such issues and a distinct feel for one's own level of racial identity are essential for the counselor leading multicultural groups. The counselor easily can be seduced into joining one or another of the coalitions formed around racial identity, which automatically augments the status and influence of that coalition (Helms, 1990). As in other counseling relationships, the group leader can have either a parallel, crossed, progressive, or regressive relationship with the group as a whole or with various coalitions within the group. The challenge of managing various coalitions of racial identity demands the highest levels of racial identity development on the part of the counselor. The chances are much greater than in individual counseling that the group leader will face the spectrum of racial identity development attitudes. A progressive relationship with some and a regressive or parallel relationship with others would seem to enhance the possibility of the group leaders joining a coalition in a deleterious fashion. In any event, the leader of a multicultural counseling group, unlike the counseling dyad, must be ready to manage various types of relationships around racial/cultural identity (Helms, 1990). The group's ability to promote the racial/cultural identity development of its members to a large extent will depend upon the leader's facility in dealing with such controversial and provocative issues of social interaction.

CASE EXAMPLE

The following group was formed at an urban counseling center:

> *Rita:* A White female, age 37 and recently divorced. She came to the counseling center because of feeling depressed and a lack of direction in her life. She works in data entry, but does not enjoy her job very much. Her WRID is assessed at the contact stage.

> *Frank:* A White male, age 40, is experiencing marital problems with his third wife, which has caused him considerable anxiety. He owns a small car dealership that earns him a decent living. His WRID is passive reintegration.

> *Bill:* A White male, age 32 and never married. He tends to be on the shy, introverted side. He has an associate degree in accounting and works at a small firm. He was referred to the group because of poor socialization. His WRID is assessed at the disintegration stage.

> *Jean:* A White female, age 45 and married. She came to counseling because of unresolved grief over her mother's death. She has a bachelor's degree in social work. Her WRID level is assessed at the pseudoindependent stage.

> *Barbara:* A Black female, age 38, a single mother. She is the executive director of a women's center. She came to counseling because of feeling very stressed out in her job. She has a degree in language and communication. Her RID (racial identity development) level is assessed at the internalization stage.

> *Michael:* A Black male, age 33. He is a salesman for a pharmaceutical company. He was referred to the counseling center by his medical doctor who found nothing wrong in spite of Michael's many somatic complaints. His RID level is assessed at the preencounter stage.

Carlos: A Hispanic male, age 50, married with children. Carlos was required to seek counseling by his supervisors because of violent outbursts at the welding company where he works. His CID (cultural identity development) level is assessed at the resistance stage.

Miriam: A Hispanic female, age 35, and also a single parent. She came to counseling because of feeling overwhelmed by problems with her children. She has her own hairstyling business, does rather well financially, and desires to expand her business. Her CID level is at the dissonance stage.

Fred: An Asian male, age 34. He recently got his college degree in computers and has gone to work for a big computer company. He is engaged to be married and first came to the counseling center because of sleep and appetite disturbance. His CID level is assessed at the conformity stage.

Jenny: An Asian female, age 30, single and lives at home with her parents. She works as a secretary for her native country's embassy. A friend referred her to the counseling center because she began having conflicts with her parents and this caused her a great deal of anxiety, to the point of crying several times a day. Her CID level is at the integrative awareness stage.

Marsha: The group leader, White, age 42. She has been working in the field of counseling for almost 15 years. She has had several years of experience running groups, but this is her first group with such diversity, which causes her some anxiety. Her WRID level is at the pseudoindependence stage.

Group Dynamics

The group has an even number (excluding the group leader) of males and females. There are four White people in the group (two males and two females), and six non-Whites: two Blacks, two Asians, and two Hispanics. If one were considering issues of race and gender without looking at differences in racial identity and forms of second-culture acquisition, one instinctively might suspect coalitions to form along the lines of males versus females and Whites versus non-Whites. This kind of diversity requires the clinician to consider other differences. For example, based on the research presented earlier, Whites in the group could be feeling quite un-comfortable as they find themselves outnumbered by non-Whites. How-ever, a closer look indicates there are two members (Fred and Michael) at the first stage of minority identity development (wanting to be like the White majority) who could easily join a coalition of White people. Now, we have a group of four Whites and two non-Whites who want to be like Whites. In addition, Jean, a pseudoindependent, might find it difficult to join the White racial attitudes of Frank, Rita, and Bill.

Regarding the other racial subgroupings, the skilled multicultural group leader will be aware that the two Blacks are at opposite ends of racial identity development and rather than form a coalition they could be extremely divergent. Michael, at the preencounter stage and desirous to be White, might "split off" his Black identity and project it onto Barbara, with the result of rejecting his Blackness through rejecting Barbara. On the other hand, Barbara, though at the internalization stage, could have a visceral reaction to Michael's conformity and projection onto her. How-ever, the assumption is that she's been through the preencounter stage herself; therefore, Barbara may be in a position to empathize with Michael and actually serve as a catalyst for the evolution of his racial identity development.

The situation that exists for Michael and Barbara is also true for the two Asians, Fred (conformity) and Jenny (integrative awareness). At one point, Fred, highly assimilated into the mainstream culture, criticized Jenny for still living at home with her parents and urged her to give up the "old ways." The more racially developed group members (Jean and Barbara) came to Jenny's defense. The group leader intervened by asking Jenny for her own reaction to Fred. Jenny, at the integrative awareness stage and able to appreciate the positives of her Asian and American identities, po-litely revealed her feeling that Fred, so desirous to be successful, found it necessary to deny his "Asianess" and assume the identity of his White counterparts. Fred was visibly shaken by Jenny's candor but, with the em-pathy of both the group leader and other members, Fred was challenged to see that part of "making it in the business world" meant receiving feed-back from others who may also be women.

Frank (a passive reintegrated White) poses two possibilities for the group: He can overpower the group by his demeanor and attitude or he can suffer annihilation by the group as the scapegoat. Frank is a very visible figure in the group and because of his racist (and sexist) attitudes can easily become the receptacle for the split-off, racist attitudes of other group members. Frank will audition well for this part. Whether Frank becomes a dominant player in the group will depend on the amount of support he can muster. This could come from members like Fred, Michael, and Rita—who are all at the earliest stage of RID—but it's not likely. If there were more reintegrated Whites in the group, Frank could very easily form a strong and overpowering coalition. However, the only member at a parallel stage of RID with Frank is Carlos (resistance), but he is Hispanic and therefore would be rejecting toward Whites. Though Carlos also evidences sexist attitudes in the group, his antipathy toward Whites most likely would prevent him from entering into a coalition with Frank.

The possibility for the strongest coalition could exist among the three women who have the highest RID (Barbara, Jean, and Jenny). Furthermore, the possibility exists that the group leader (also a woman and a pseudoindependent White) could join this coalition. If this were to happen, the coalition could assume a force alienating to the rest of the group members. The skilled group leader must be aware of this seductive pull and avoid its temptation so as not to create feelings of abandonment in the other group members.

Carlos (a resistant Hispanic) and Bill (a disintegrated White) are most at-risk for deep-seated feelings of isolation and consequential premature termination. Bill is shy and reserved by nature, and Frank has already interrogated him as to why he is single and has no girlfriends. It was fairly obvious to the group that Frank was insinuating that Bill could be gay. However, every group has a rescuer and savior, and Rita, a contact White, nurtures and protects Bill. The group in its working stage has begun to see this dynamic and use it to provide helpful feedback to both Bill and Rita. Carlos, on the other hand, is terribly isolated in the group and frequently misses sessions. He sees Miriam (a dissonant Hispanic) as his only ally in the group. However, in her confused state, she is put off by Carlos's anger and at times macho attitude and is more drawn to the other women in the group. The group leader must tread delicately with Carlos, allowing him to feel that what he has to say is important and bolstering his receptivity to feedback from other members of the group.

There are an infinite number of scenarios around racial/cultural identity issues that can take place in a group of this kind. Hopefully, after this brief exposition, the counselor leading multicultural groups will combine the racial/cultural identity and second-culture acquisition paradigms with more traditional ones to achieve a greater understanding of the many dynamics that can take place in groups and, most especially, in groups of cultural diversity.

SUMMARY

This chapter has integrated some of the more dynamic principles of group counseling with the constructs of second-culture acquisition and cultural identity development. Groups can be structured or nonstructured, homogeneous or heterogeneous. Less structured and more heterogeneous groups generate greater anxiety among members allowing them to not so consciously take on roles and engage in the common defense mechanism of projective identification. In groups of greater cultural diversity, minority group membership will play a large part in the development of group roles and projections. The case example illustrated how members of dominant or nondominant status outside the group and their level of cultural identity development will create challenges for even the most skilled counselor. However, multiculturally skilled group leaders will understand these challenges as potentially enriching for both the group members and themselves. The key to successful group counseling is the constructive use of anxiety, especially that generated by cultural differences.

REFERENCES

Acosta, F.X., & Yamamoto, J. (1984). The utility of group work practice for Hispanic Americans. *Social Work with Groups, 7,* 63–73.

Alonso, A., & Rutan, J.S. (1984). The impact of object relations theory on psychodynamic group therapy. *American Journal of Psychiatry, 141,* 1376–1380.

Bion, W.R. (1961). *Experience in groups.* New York: Basic Books.

Brown, J.A. (1984). Group work with low-income Black youths. *Social Work with Groups, 7,* 111–124.

Burke, A.W. (1984). The outcome of the multi-racial small group experience. *International Journal of Social Psychiatry, 30,* 96–101.

Chu, J., & Sue, S. (1984). Asian/Pacific-Americans and group practice. *Social Work with Groups, 7,* 23–26.

Comas-Diaz, L. (1984). Content themes in group treatment with Puerto Rican women. *Social Work with Groups, 7,* 75–84.

Davis, L. (1979). Racial composition of groups. *Journal for Specialists in Group Work, 24,* 208–213.

Davis, L.E. (1984). Essential components of group work with Black Americans. *Social Work with Groups, 7,* 97–109.

Edwards, E.D., & Edwards, M.E. (1984). Group work practice with American Indians. *Social Work with Groups, 7,* 7–21.

Egan, G. (1973). *Face to face: The small group experience and interpersonal growth.* Pacific Grove, CA: Brooks/Cole.

Freud, S. (1958). The dynamics of transference. In J. Strachey (Ed. and Trans.), *The standard edition of the complete psychological works of Sigmund Freud* (Vol. 12, pp. 97–108). London: Hogarth Press. (Original work published 1912)

Greeley, A.T., Garcia, V.L., Kessler, B.L., & Gilchrest, G. (1992). Training effective multicultural group counselors: Issues for a group training course. *Journal for Specialists in Group Work, 17,* 196–209.

Helms, J.E. (1990). Generalizing racial identity interaction theory to groups. In J.E. Helms (Ed.), *Black and White racial identity* (pp. 187–204). Westport, CT: Greenwood.

Ho, M.K. (1984). Social group work with Asian/Pacific Americans. *Social Work with Groups, 7,* 49–61.

Jackson, S. (1992). Team composition in organizational settings: Issues in managing an increasingly diverse workforce. In S. Worchel, W. Wood, & J. Simpson (Eds.), *Group process and productivity* (pp. 138–173). Newbury Park, CA: Sage.

Jacobs, E.E., Harvill, R.L., & Masson, R.L. (1994). *Group counseling: Strategies and skills.* Pacific Grove, CA: Brooks/Cole.

Janis, I.L. (1982). *Groupthink: Psychological studies on policy decision.* Boston: Houghton-Mifflin.

Johnson, D.W., & Johnson, F.P. (1994). *Joining together: Group theory and group skills.* Boston: Allyn and Bacon.

Klein, M. (1946). Notes on some schizoid mechanisms. *International Journal of Psychoanalysis, 27,* 99–110.

Lee, P.C., Juan, G., & Hom, A.B. (1984). Group work practice with Asian clients: A sociocultural approach. *Social Work with Groups, 7,* 37–48.

McRoy, R.G., & Oglesby, Z. (1984). Group work with Black adoptive applicants. *Social Work with Groups, 7,* 125–134.

Merta, R.J. (1995). Group work: Multicultural perspectives. In J.G. Ponterotto, J.M. Casas, L.A. Suzuki, & C.M. Alexander (Eds.), *Handbook of multicultural counseling* (pp. 567–585). Thousand Oaks, CA: Sage.

Shields, J.D., & Lanza, M.L. (1993). The parallel process of resistance by clients and therapists to starting groups: A guide for nurses. *Archives of Psychiatric Nursing, 7,* 300–307.

Sullivan, H.S. (1953). *The interpersonal theory of psychiatry.* New York: W.W. Norton.

Wells, L. (1990). The group as a whole: A systemic socioanalytic perspective on interpersonal and group relations. In J. Gillete & M. McCollom (Eds.), *Groups in context* (pp. 49–85). Reading, MA: Addison-Wesley.

Wheelan, S.A. (1994). *Group processes: A developmental perspective.* Boston: Allyn and Bacon.

Yalom, I.D. (1995). *The theory and practice of group psychotherapy.* New York: Basic Books.

Zinner, J. (1976). The implications of projective identification for marital interaction. In H. Grunebaum & J. Christ (Eds.), *Contemporary marriage: Structure, dynamics, and therapy* (pp. 293–308). Boston: Little, Brown.

—⚜—

MULTICULTURAL FAMILY COUNSELING

FAMILY COUNSELING

Just as group counseling is promoted by the advantages of seeing the individual in a social microcosm, so, too, family counseling emphasizes the need for understanding the individual in a wider context—namely, that of the family system. Since multicultural counseling also emphasizes the wider context, that of culture, the blending of these two movements creates a powerful treatment strategy. With its emphasis upon the contextual and the systemic, family counseling has a natural affinity to multi-culturalism.

The Family Counseling Movement

One way of understanding the development of family counseling is to contrast it with psychoanalysis. Freud, much like evolutionary anthropologists who sought to understand humans in terms of their forebears, believed that a complete understanding of the individual could only take place by searching and studying, out of context, events in a person's past. In contrast, the family counseling movement began by trying to understand the here-and-now function of a member's behavior in the family system. Historical investigation and understanding of behavior were much less important than seeing how such behavior served the larger context. Family counseling sought to replace an evolutionary view of behavior with a functional one; it was an attempt to explain behavior as adaptive to the larger environment. While psychoanalysis had insisted on treating the individual in isolation in order to manipulate behavior understood as internally organized, family counseling seeks to treat the entire family system in order to alter patterns of family interaction seen as the dominant forces in personality development.

Fundamental Concepts in Family Counseling

From this basic notion of functionalism and systems thinking, certain important concepts in family counseling evolved and endure to the present day.

Homeostasis. All systems seek homeostasis, "the tendency of a system to regulate itself so as to maintain a constant internal environment in response to changes in external environment" (Nichols & Schwartz, 1995, p. 90). Though overly mechanistic in its purely conceptual form, homeostasis, when applied to families, means that at times symptomatic behaviors can be understood as regulating the family system and protecting it from a perceived external threat. A typical example is a child who develops school phobia after his or her mother returns from an operation in the hospital. The threat of illness is counteracted by the child's constant vigilance of the mother. The concept of homeostasis has been much criticized by contemporary family counselors as fostering an overly mechanistic view of families. This criticism is valid, as no family system is so mechanical. Nevertheless, the concept of homeostasis provides family practitioners with a useful tool in assessing the effects of symptomatic behavior upon the family system.

Circularity. In opposition to a linear understanding of behavior that searches for explanations in the past, the concept of circularity views behavior within a system as reverberating, circling, or looping around—thus creating patterns of interaction and communication. The linear equation of A causes B is replaced by A affecting B in turn affecting A. Take the example of a punitive father and his acting-out son. The son's acting out causes the father to be punitive, which in turn causes further acting out on the son's part. A good family counselor becomes skilled at tracking the interaction and communication patterns of a family through their enactment in a family counseling session. By using the concept of circularity, the counselor can intervene effectively to interrupt such patterns.

Family Structure. Concern with family structure emanated from two great pioneers in the field of family counseling: J. Haley (1963, 1976) and Salvador Minuchin (Minuchin & Fishman, 1981; Minuchin, Montalvo, Guerney, Rosman, & Schumer, 1967). Haley, a member of the Mental Research Institute (MRI) in Palo Alto, California, became concerned with issues of power and control in families and viewed behavior as a function of these two ends. This, in turn, led to the concepts of hierarchy, subsystems, boundaries, and coalitions. A healthy family has a parental subsystem functioning as the hierarchy, with clear boundaries around the subsystems. However, to illustrate structural dysfunction, a mother who is having difficulties in the relationship with her husband can enter into a coalition with one or more of the children against the father in order to lessen his authority and influence. Minuchin capitalized on Haley and classified family boundaries as rigid, clear, or diffuse and leading to interpersonal relationships that are either disengaged, normal, or enmeshed. Structural family counselors are known for their creative and strategic techniques aimed at restructuring a family in order to create a functional hierarchy with a clear boundary around itself and the sibling subsystem.

Triangulation. Murray Bowen (1976) introduced the concept of triangles into family counseling to illustrate a lack of differentiation among family members. Bowen believed fusion among family members to be a chief cause of symptomatic behavior. When two undifferentiated people in a relationship face anxiety, there is a tendency to draw in a third party as a way of reducing the couple's anxiety. In families, this usually takes the form of children being triangulated into conflicts between their parents. A triangulated person is not allowed to differentiate, which in turn can lead to symptomatic behavior. Thus, family counselors recognize that a daughter's behavior depends on her relationship with her mother, which depends on Mother's relationship with her husband. Bowen believed all behavior to be basically triadic rather than dyadic.

These are some of the basic concepts of family systems counseling that are still very much used today. An understanding of these basic ideas will facilitate their multicultural application to family counseling.

Fundamentals of Treatment

There are many schools of family counseling, each with its own set of strategies and techniques. Therefore, it is somewhat risky to give a list of treatment fundamentals that transcends individual schools of thought. However, given the goals of the present chapter and my own identification as a structural family counselor, an understanding of the following treatment fundamentals of family counseling is necessary.

Joining. As in most traditional forms of counseling, a part of joining in family work requires the development of a working relationship with the family. However, unlike traditional forms of counseling, joining can also be strategic. The family counselor can choose to join the family in different ways by establishing a coalition with one or more family members in order, for example, to involve an underfunctioning member or to undermine a dysfunctional coalition in the system. The counselor's joining can vary during the course of treatment, given the needs of the system. For example, a counselor may join initially with a father who has been excluded for whatever reason from the executorship of the family. Later on, the counselor may join with the mother in her efforts to share the executorship with the father, who may be resisting his responsibility.

Enactment. Rather than talking to individual members of the family system, here the counselor's task is to effectuate a family "enactment"—an interaction of family members among themselves for purposes of assessing patterns of communication and planning interventions to block or disrupt dysfunctional patterns. The assumption behind enactment is that, given the proper coaching, family members inevitably will behave in the counseling room as they do at home. Criticizing enacted patterns is not enough, as the counselor must also give the family alternatives and coach them to enact such options right there in the counseling room. Enactment is to family counseling what transference is to psychoanalysis (G. Simon, personal communication, February 1995).

Boundary Making. From Minuchin's idea that dysfunctional families are either enmeshed or disengaged comes the technique of boundary making—designed to separate family members who are too close and bring together those who are too distant (Nichols & Schwartz, 1995). For example, the counselor may encourage two disengaged members to begin interacting, which inevitably will evoke interruption from a third party. The counselor's task is to actively block such interruptions, allowing the disengaged members to form more functional boundaries.

Reframing. In its most basic form, reframing is the counselors helping a family to view a problem in a different way. Though not particular to family counseling—as one could argue that all counseling is about changing perception—reframing has become a favorite tool of family systems work. A typical reframe to a parent of a child's problematic behavior might be: "I think your daughter's opposition is her way of being close to you."

Though by no means an exhaustive list, these treatment fundamentals are common terminology in family counseling and can be integrated into multicultural interventions with families.

Contemporary Criticisms of Family Counseling

Before proceeding to multicultural counseling of families, it is necessary to examine some contemporary criticisms of family counseling. These criticisms are divided into four: constructivism, feminism, psychoeducation, and multiculturalism.

Constructivism. Constructivism is a new epistemology that maintains that what is known as real is merely a construction of the observer. Since individuals are constructed of their own biases, assumptions, and cultural determinants, there is no one given truth about reality. Rather, there is construction of reality, whose meaning can vary from person to person, group to group, culture to culture. Thus, the task of the family counselor is to collaborate with a family in the search for meaning of present behaviors and alternate meanings for the same behaviors. The constructivist critique undermines traditional family counseling because of its tendency to impose upon families a universally accepted truth about how they ought to function, and to focus on actions rather than meanings.

Feminism. Similar to constructivism, the feminist critique also accuses traditional family counseling of treating families out of context. Family counseling by and large ignored the historical and societal context of women that encouraged them to desire positions of economic dependency and domesticity over responsibility. Family counselors, themselves steeped in patriarchy, tended to view such roles as pathological, and the solution was to have the man (father) of the family come to the rescue by assuming a more involved role in the family. Feminists reacted strongly to this pathologizing of women and the power-assuming position of the counselor, which only replicated society's inequality between men and women. Like the contructivists, the feminists promote a kinder, gentler way of working with families.

Psychoeducation. Psychoeducation, in its approach to families with a disturbed member, is antithetical to traditional family counseling in that it viewed the family system as victim of the behavior. The family counseling movement tended to blame the system for creating symptomatic behavior. For psychoeducators, this was blaming the victim. For example, in working with the family of a schizophrenic, the best form of counseling is to educate the family about the disease and give them better resources in how to deal with it. In theories of psychoeducational counseling, if there was dysfunction in the family system it was caused primarily by not knowing how to deal with a disturbed member. Thus, the illness causes the family system to dysfunction—not the system causing the illness, as traditional family counseling would have us believe.

Multiculturalism. The family counseling movement suffered still another blow in the 1980s from multicultural counseling, which accused it of being Eurocentric. The depiction of the healthy family appeared to be based upon a particular culture, that of the White American middle class. There was little regard for how family systems could vary across cultures or how family structure, considered dysfunctional in one culture, would not be in another. The 1980s saw a dramatic rise in different kinds of family structures: the single-parent family, grandmother as primary caretaker, and homosexual couples raising children. This, together with the steady increase of non-White immigrants to the United States, created a challenge for traditional family counseling—which tended to impose universally upon families values that are culture-specific. This debate between the multiculturalists and the structuralists continues into the 1990s and shows no signs of abating. The structuralists have reworked their position to say, for example, that issues of disengagement and enmeshment exist in all families, regardless of culture. However, culture would define the degree to which such relationships are tolerable. For example, one would not impose the same standard of enmeshment upon an Iowa farm family and a Latino family.

All of the foregoing critiques have in common the belief that traditional family counseling is too myopic in its vision of families. The family therapy movement began by trying to understand individuals in their wider context, that of the family system. Ironically, beginning in the late 1980s and continuing into the 1990s, family therapy has been accused of being too narrow, of not considering the wider contexts of race, gender, ethnicity, and culture.

Szapocznik and Kurtines (1993) suggest seeing the relationship between the individual, family, and culture as concentric circles. The individual continues to be understood within the context of family, and family is understood within the context of culture. Issues of hierarchy, communication, family values, family roles, and intergenerational perspective still dominate the work of family counselors who are multiculturally sensitive. While family process may be the same across cultures, the content will vary considerably, and sensitivity to these variations will define the competent multicultural family counselor.

Moving from the fundamentals of family counseling and recent critiques, next is a vision of multicultural family counseling that is faithful to the fundamentals and sensitive to the critiques.

MULTICULTURAL FAMILY COUNSELING

In the previous two chapters, the constructs of second-culture acquisition and racial identity development were applied to both the individual and group modalities of counseling. Here, the same will take place with family counseling. The previous emphasis on intragroup differences as equally important as intergroup differences is even more true for families, where the forms of second-culture acquisition and levels of identity development may be different among family members. Though the focus of this chapter is on intrafamilial differences, this is not meant to minimize interfamilial differences. Family counselors working cross-culturally have an ethical and clinical responsibility to inform themselves through reading, supervision, workshops, and the like of the broad lines of family organization and function in a particular client's culture of origin.

While the focus of the following discussion is around the immigrant families who comprised most of my family counseling experience, many of these issues can be applied to families who do not have immigrant status. Families with nondominant status, yet whose members have had previous generations living in the United States (Black and Native American, for example), will confront many of the same issues in relation to the dominant culture.

The Immigrant Family

Sluzki (1979) developed a five-stage model for a family in migration: the preparatory stage, the act of migration, period of overcompensation, period of decompensation or crisis, and transgenerational impact. According to Sluzki, each of these stages involves different conflicts for the family and requires different coping mechanisms. Thus, a starting point for the multicultural family counselor is to ask: Where is this family in the process of cultural transition? The counselor needs to access some basic information as to when the act of migration took place and whether all members of the family system migrated together. Because of visa regulations and other conflicts in their country of origin, an increasing phenomenon in multicultural family counseling is working with families in which parents and children have been reunited after years of separation (Sciarra, 1999). Such scenarios challenge the more common display of second-culture acquisition where the children more quickly acquire characteristics of the dominant culture. If a parent(s) has preceded the children in the act of migration, the parent may be more integrated into mainstream culture than the children.

It is in Sluzki's last stage of transgenerational conflict that many immigrant families present for counseling. Here, the classic generation conflict in families is better understood through the lens of second-culture acquisition.

Second-Culture Aquisition in Families

Multicultural family counseling demands an awareness that family members will acculturate differently. Children, who because of their facility in learning the language and more frequent contacts through school and the like, generally more easily assume characteristics of the dominant culture than their parents. Parents, on the other hand, are often more closely allied with the culture of the country of origin. As time goes on, these differences may become minimized as parents more slowly acquire aspects of the dominant culture. On the contrary, the rift between parents and children can widen if parents withdraw from the dominant culture and children continue to become more allied with it, causing conflict between the subsystems. With such conflict, some immigrant families will present for counseling.

Assessment of Second-Culture Acquisition Issues. The first task of the multicultural family counselor is to assess the second-culture acquisition process of the various family members. One of the easiest ways to do this is through language (Sciarra & Ponterotto, 1993). What language does the family speak? Do the children prefer to speak in English? Do the parents speak or try to speak in English or insist on using their native language? If spoken to by their parents in their native language, do the children answer in the same language or switch to English? If counselors are bilingual, even more possibilities exist for assessment as they can switch from one language to another in addressing different family members in order to observe in what language they respond. As a bilingual

(Spanish) family counselor, my experience has been that, when I speak to the children in Spanish, they answer in English in spite of knowing Spanish. Whether they do this also with their parents is very important to assess. The following vignette illustrates some of the dynamics around language and second-culture acquisition.

> Mr. M, though poorly, attempts to speak in English to his two sons, who speak better English than Spanish. Mrs. M, on the other hand, does not speak any English, in spite of knowing a little.

From a systems point of view, one could hypothesize that Mr. M is in a coalition with his sons against his wife. From a second-culture acquisition point of view, one could assess the children as more identified with the dominant culture; Mrs. M as not identified or withdrawn from the dominant culture; and Mr. M with a willingness to become more identified with the dominant culture. Surely, the counselor will investigate further to define issues of second-culture acquisition; nevertheless, acute observation of the use of language in an initial session can give the counselor a map of the family system to be used for further exploration.

Another way to assess the degree of second-culture acquisition in families is to gather information about celebration of holidays and food. Does the family continue to eat ethnic food? Do the children complain about having to eat such food? Are holidays of the dominant or nondominant culture—or both—celebrated? Are special days of the week reserved to maintain traditions of the nondominant culture? Frank is a good example of these kinds of issues.

> Frank is a recent Italian immigrant and father of four. He works long hours, six days a week, in a grocery store. Sunday is the only day he can spend with his family, and as in his native country Frank feels the Sunday meal is very important. Frank wants his children present for the big noonday, Sunday meal, which will continue for several hours accompanied by relaxing and talking with extended family members. Through their contacts at school, two of Frank's children have become involved in a soccer league, and many of the games are on Sunday. Though Frank likes the idea of his children playing soccer, he resents their refusal to be present at the Sunday meal. Frank cannot understand why Americans put games at times that interfere with family. The children, on the other hand, can't understand why they

have to be home on Sunday for so many hours when no one else does that. Frank feels his children are disrespectful.

In this scenario, levels of acculturation are revealed more through adherence, or lack thereof, to the customs of the native country. This kind of information gathering and observation of interactional patterns among family members is a form of enactment—a strategy so important to traditional family counseling. The skilled multicultural counselor also employs enactment but filters the information through the lens of second-culture acquisition. The counselor is asking: How is what I am seeing and hearing revealing the acculturative level of the family system, along with different forms of second-culture acquisition among its members?

Treatment of Conflicting Forms of Second-Culture Acquisition. When intergenerational conflict can be reframed as intercultural conflict, Szapocznik, Santisteban, Kurtines, Perez-Vidal, and Hervis (1984) suggested a psychoeducational approach, which they have termed "Bicultural Effectiveness Training" (BET). The BET approach is unique in that it utilizes some of the fundamentals of family systems theory and reframes them in terms of intercultural conflict. For example, systems theory posits that symptomatic behavior serves a function for the system. In family counseling, that becomes translated into the creation of the identified patient (IP), who is given individual blame for what is really a systemic problem. Szapocznik et al. (1984) suggest that culture be labeled as the IP, thereby taking the blame off any one individual in the family and making culture the repository of the family's dysfunction. A parent-child conflict is reframed as conflict between cultures in which each member has a point of view that is culturally determined (Szapocznik & Kurtines, 1993). The following is a possible counselor reframe in culturally sensitive family counseling:

> I do not believe that your children disrespect you. What I believe is that they are trying to give you something of value and at the same time asking you to give them something of value. I believe this something to be your different cultural understandings and appreciations.

In a second moment, BET encourages a different kind of interaction whereby parents and children can be given the opportunity to hear, understand, and accept the value of certain aspects of each others' culture

(Szapocznik, Rio, Perez-Vidal, Kurtines, Hervis, & Santisteban, 1986). Parents listen and learn to appreciate from their children American culture; children, on the other hand, listen and learn to appreciate their parent's culture. When one is working with immigrant families, intergenerational conflict should be reframed as intercultural. The task of the family counselor is to facilitate a "multiculturalism" within the family, or as Szapocznik et al. (1984) prefer, to convert the family from intergenerational dysfunction to bicultural effectiveness.

Returning to the example of Frank, BET would encourage Frank to learn from his children the positive aspects of American culture. His children in turn would listen to Frank about Italian culture, hopefully detouring them from the road of further alienation. A common scenario of intergenerational conflict in immigrant families involves dating habits of adolescent daughters. American culture, allowing females to date unchaperoned as early as age 14 and 15, is generally seen as too permissive by immigrant parents. It is fairly easy to reframe this kind of conflict as intercultural. Give the parents an opportunity to describe the dating customs in their native country. (Most adolescents listen with a great deal of curiosity.) Then, ask the adolescent to react, giving the pros and cons of such customs. In turn, allow the parents to listen to their children about the dating customs in American culture and ask them for their reaction. The multicultural family counselor must always be guided by the potential richness of such interaction. If the counselor can move the family away from seeing the problem as one of authority and obedience to seeing an opportunity for mutual enrichment, a major step toward successful treatment has been accomplished.

Bilingualism in the Treatment Process

If language is a primary indicator of second-culture acquisition form, then the counselor can use the family's bilingualism in service of the counseling process. Sciarra and Ponterotto (1993) wrote about the difficulty of enforcing the one-language rule upon families. Typical of the immigrant families with whom I have worked, all members spoke the native language, with parents speaking little or no English and the children being bilingual. Since many of the families were Latino, I have had the luxury of being a subordinate bilingual (speaking Spanish but dominant in English). In the initial work with these families, a rational approach was taken with the insistence that all speak in Spanish, since that would obviate the need for translation. Children tended to resist such an imposition, with the realization that the use of language had to be understood more dynamically. Children's refusal to speak in their native language could be thought of in structural terms as separation from parents, or in acculturative terms as identification with the dominant culture. Thus, if counselors are bilingual, they can switch from one language to another as determined by the therapeutic goal. For example, if they wish to shore up a coalition with the parents, speaking in the native language would be indicated. On the contrary, if the goal is to promote the children's identification with the dominant culture or to solidify a boundary around the sibling subsystem, speaking in English would be more indicated. If the counselor is not bilingual and there is the need for one family member to translate for another, similar dynamics apply. Which family member the counselor chooses to translate for another family member can be guided by structural concerns. Consider the following example.

> Mr. J is a monolingual Spanish-speaking father. Mrs. J is bilingual, dominant in Spanish. Their son and daughter are bilingual, dominant in English. Mrs. J tends to overfunction while Mr. J appears uninvolved and marginalized. In the early sessions, Mrs. J spontaneously translates for her husband.

Here, the counselor can intervene by blocking Mrs. J and requesting that her son translate for Mr. J. This intervention serves a dual purpose: It reduces Mrs. J's level of functioning and establishes more of a connection between Mr. J and his son. On the structural level, the goal is to reduce Mr. J's marginal position by establishing a father-son connection. On the acculturative level, the counselor can promote bicultural effectiveness between father and son.

In the bilingual family where it is assumed that there are various forms of second-culture acquisition, language can be used dynamically by both monolingual and bilingual counselors to realign the structure of the family and to promote bicultural effectiveness.

Cultural Identity Development (CID) and Multicultural Family Counseling

As has been the format in previous chapters, the CID model is now applied to family systems.

Assessment. Gushue (1993), in a seminal article, was the first to apply the CID model to families. He suggests a tripolar mapping of families to include the counselor, the parental subsystem, and the sibling subsystem (Figure 6.1). However, the counselor is not limited to these three polarities. For example, an extended family member(s) may form a fourth polarity. Unlike the dyad in individual counseling, family counseling presents several polarities from which to assess parallel, regressive, or progressive relationships. Through the methods discussed in Chapter 3, it is important for counselors to assess the CID level of the family members and to have a keen sense of their own CID level. Let us look at a number of possible scenarios.

As previously seen, progressive relationships, in general, offer a better prognosis for treatment than either regressive or parallel relationships. Family counseling is no exception; however, the dynamics are more complicated. For example, an autonomy stage counselor from a dominant cultural group will enjoy a progressive relationship with parents and siblings from a nondominant cultural group who are at the conformity and resistance stages, respectively (see Figure 6.2).

The prognosis for treatment is good. However, since the counselor's CID level is closer to that of the siblings (the parents being at the first stage of development), he or she must be careful of entering into a coalition with the children against the parents. In actuality, this could be a non-White family whose executive subsystem accepts the ways of the dominant culture. The members of the sibling subsystem are taking a good deal of pride in their own culture and rejecting the ways of the dominant culture. As does the paradigm of second-culture acquisition, CID can frame this conflict of the immigrant family in terms of differing attitudes toward the dominant and nondominant cultures. Parents in this scenario who complain about the opposition of their children can be told something like the following:

—⊸◐◑◐⊷—

FIGURE 6.1 *A Tripolar Family Map*

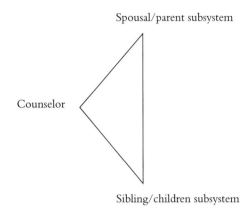

Spousal/parent subsystem

Counselor

Sibling/children subsystem

—⊸◐◑◐⊷—

FIGURE 6.2 *Dominant-Culture Counselor/Nondominant-Culture Family*

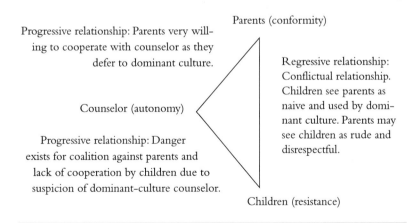

Parents (conformity)

Progressive relationship: Parents very will-ing to cooperate with counselor as they defer to dominant culture.

Regressive relationship: Conflictual relationship. Children see parents as naive and used by domi-nant culture. Parents may see children as rude and disrespectful.

Counselor (autonomy)

Progressive relationship: Danger exists for coalition against parents and lack of cooperation by children due to suspicion of dominant-culture counselor.

Children (resistance)

> I do not think your children dislike you. I believe that they are asking for your help in how to relate in a world that they feel does not like Black people.

The counselor, using the CID model, is able to reframe the conflict in terms of attitude toward the dominant culture. Another challenge for counselors in this scenario is tolerating the hostility toward themselves generated by feelings associated with the resistance stage. The counselor from the dominant culture will always be seen by those at the resistance stage as the embodiment of that against which they are rebelling.

If, in the above scenario, a nondominant counselor at the conformity stage were substituted, the prognosis for treatment is not good. The counselor has a parallel relationship with the parents and a regressive relationship with the children (Figure 6.3). A real danger exists for a coalition between counselor and parents against the children. Furthermore, the counselor does not enjoy a level of CID sufficient to handle the suspicion and hostility characterized by the children's resistance stage. On the other hand, counselors from a nondominant culture at the awareness stage would be able to handle such hostility toward themselves and also be able to reframe such hostility toward the parents from a CID perspective.

Treatment. Unlike the paradigm of second-culture acquisition CID places more of an emphasis upon development that can occur only through lived experience. One moves out of the conformity to the dissonance stage, for example, by having an experience of racism. For example, a higher stage of CID for children is a result of their having experiences of the relationship between the dominant and nondominant culture that their parents do not share. Culturally sensitive family counseling will try to access those experiences and use them for enactment material. For example, the counselor can say:

> Tina, it's quite obvious that you feel differently toward White people than your parents. Can you help them to understand what experiences have led you to such feelings?

An intervention such as this will allow the family to enact its disagreements around the relationship to the dominant culture. The challenge

FIGURE 6.3 *Nondominant-Culture Counselor/ Nondominant-Culture Family*

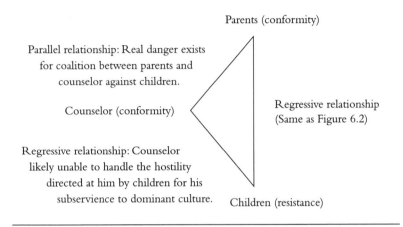

Parents (conformity)

Parallel relationship: Real danger exists
for coalition between parents and
counselor against children.

Counselor (conformity)

Regressive relationship
(Same as Figure 6.2)

Regressive relationship: Counselor
likely unable to handle the hostility
directed at him by children for his
subservience to dominant culture.

Children (resistance)

when working with a family system where the children and counselor are at a higher level of CID than the parents is to avoid undermining the executive subsystem. The same is true within the paradigm of second-culture acquisition when children are more integrated into the dominant culture and speak its language. In the immigrant family, children may be prone to looking down upon their parents for their lack of biculturalism and/or their naivete around issues of prejudice against minority groups. How does the counselor respect the children's development while at the same time shore up the executive subsystem? This is a delicate challenge. First, the counselor needs to keep the focus on the different experiences of the family members that have led to differing attitudes. Second, the counselor should emphasize that by listening one does not give up power and authority. For example, one could intervene in the following fashion:

> Mrs. G, you are in charge of this family. You have the final say as to what goes on here. And being in charge brings with it the burden of listening carefully to the experiences of all members of the family.

I'd like you now to listen carefully to your daughter's experience of White people and then I would like you to respond.

The goal of this intervention is to validate different attitudes among family members while at the same time affirming the parent's rightful place as executor.

Family structure, second-culture acquisition, and CID are three useful constructs that can be employed by the multicultural family counselor. This chapter ends with a case example that attempts to integrate the three.

CASE EXAMPLE

Figure 6.4 is a genogram of the Rodriguez family, who has presented for counseling because of Ricky's behavioral problems in school. School personnel have informed the parents that Ricky, previously a good student, has begun hanging around with the wrong crowd. Several months ago, Awilda's mother and son from a previous marriage came from their native country to live with the family.

Assessment

After two sessions of enacting family interaction and using the family structure, second-culture acquisition, and CID paradigms, the following assessment was made.

> *Jose:* Ricky's father. At present, exhibits a good deal of anger. He has worked hard doing factory work the last 15 years since coming to the United States. He feels that he and his Latino colleagues are treated unfairly by their White bosses. Though fairly integrated into mainstream culture, he now wishes to return to his native country. He is bilingual, subordinate in English; his CID level is assessed at the resistance stage.

> *Awilda:* Ricky's mother. Has recently begun working as a social work assistant after graduating from a two-year community college. She is well integrated into the dominant culture, is fluently bilingual, and

—◦◦◦—

FIGURE 6.4 *Genogram of the Rodriguez Family*

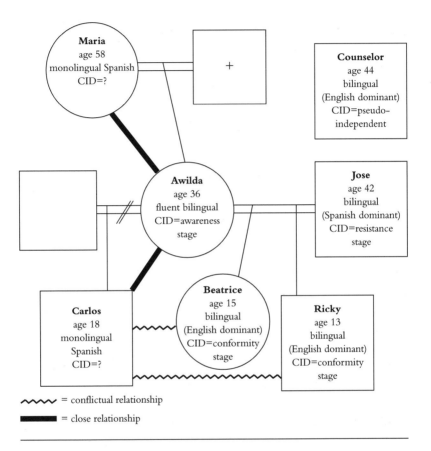

having attended an urban college with a diverse population has an appreciation of her own and different cultures. Her CID level is assessed at the awareness stage. She does not share her husband's desire to return to their native country.

Beatrice and Ricky: Born in the United States, they have assimilated the dominant culture. They are bilingual, subordinate in Spanish, and show a lack of desire to speak Spanish in the family sessions. Most of their friends are White and they attend a predominantly White school. Their CID level is assessed at the conformity stage.

Maria: The maternal grandmother recently arrived from her native country. She is monolingual Spanish and has little or no contact with the dominant culture. She spends her time mainly caring for the household and with Spanish-speaking women her own age.

Carlos: Natural son of Awilda and stepson to Jose. Also recently arrived and monolingual Spanish. He began attending a bilingual school program but has had trouble adjusting.

Counselor: Is a White male, bilingual, subordinate in Spanish, and self-assessed at the pseudoindependent stage of WRID.

Dynamics

On a structural level, it appears that the executive subsystem has been undermined due to Awilda's entrance into the workforce and her mother's entrance into the family system. Decisions previously made between Awilda and Jose are now made between Awilda and her mother. Awilda tries hard to make her mother and her son's adaptation to the United States a successful one. There appears to be a strong bond among the three. Awilda's diverted attention could be the reason for Ricky's behavioral symptoms. Ricky and Beatrice appear to have bonded in their antipathy toward Carlos, who reminds them of a culture and way of living from which they wish to distance themselves. Jose and Ricky have a conflictual relationship. Jose shows little understanding for Ricky's problems and says the solution lies in his staying away from White boys. The counselor has more of an affinity with Awilda, as she appears strong, resourceful, and willing to work on family problems. Jose, on the other hand, directs some of his anger, as expected, toward the White counselor. He is inclined to make remarks such as: "I don't know why we're here"; "This is a waste of time"; and "Things are only getting worse." Because of the CID levels among Awilda, Jose, and the counselor, it would be facile for the counselor to enter into a coalition with Awilda, as he also feels the need to pull Maria and more so Carlos into the family sessions.

Goal and Interventions

From a structural viewpoint, a revitalization of the executive subsystem is the primary goal. Ricky needs to see that, in spite of his parents' differing attitudes toward the dominant culture, they still can work together in dealing with their children. Theoretically, Awilda, at the awareness stage, can empathize with her husband's feelings of the resistance stage, having been there herself. The counselor should encourage an enactment around these issues and needs to observe Maria's comportment during the dialogue between Awilda and Jose. If there is some interference on her part, it needs to be treated delicately. Maria cannot be allowed to undermine Awilda and Jose. On the other hand, she is a key player whom the counselor must be careful not to alienate. At times, she can be called upon as a "consultant" to help with appropriate family matters. Whenever there are adult kinship members involved in the family system (as may be the case with many immigrant families), the counselor must take their roles seriously.

As a second goal, the counselor needs to take seriously the relationship between Jose and Ricky. This can be difficult because of their CID levels, Ricky at the conformity stage and Jose at the resistance stage. Jose typically views Ricky's opposition as pure disobedience. However, if the counselor can introduce the theme of culture and their different relationships to the dominant culture, a more meaningful avenue of interaction can be opened. The assumption is that Jose was also once at the conformity stage. He came to the United States with great hopes for himself and his family and at the beginning felt he had to deny his cultural background in order to move ahead. Having discovered the erroneousness of such an attitude, he is particularly susceptible to a son who evidences a similar attitude. In this situation, the counselor could encourage Jose to speak about his early years in the United States, with the goal of having him realize that his son's attitude is a necessary step in Ricky's development.

Finally, the overfunctioning of Awilda toward both Maria and Carlos needs to be tamed as it adversely affects both her husband and her other children, who may miss the diverted attention. In this situation, the counselor can once again resort to Jose's CID level (resistance to the dominant culture) and Maria's isolation from the dominant culture to effectuate a bond between the two. Jose can receive from Maria, a recent arrival, a more realistic picture of their native country—which may either diminish or augment his desire to return. The hope is that Awilda's perseverance and higher CID level will help to facilitate Jose's progression from the resistance stage. This would be a significant development in the family system, as it would strengthen the executive subsystem, facilitate a rapprochement between father and son, and contribute to Carlos's integration into the dominant culture.

SUMMARY

This case example is an attempt at illustrating how one can think about the structure of a family using the constructs of second-culture acquisition and CID. It does not mean to be exhaustive in its representation of assessment, goals, and interventions. However, it is meant to provide the reader with a culturally sensitive framework within which to think about families from diverse cultures.

REFERENCES

Bowen, M. (1976). Theory in the practice of psychotherapy. In P.J. Guerin (Ed.), *Family therapy: Theory and practice*. New York: Gardner.

Gushue, G.V. (1993). Cultural identity development and family assessment: An interaction model. *The Counseling Psychologist, 21,* 487–513.

Haley, J. (1963). *Strategies of psychotherapy.* New York: Grune and Stratton.

Haley, J. (1976). *Problem-solving therapy.* San Francisco: Jossey-Bass.

Minuchin, S., & Fishman, H.C. (1981). *Family therapy techniques.* Cambridge, MA: Harvard University Press.

Minuchin, S., Montalvo, B., Guerney, B., Rosman, B., & Schumer, F. (1967). *Families of the slums.* New York: Basic Books.

Nichols, M.P., & Schwartz, R.C. (1995). *Family therapy: Concepts and methods.* Boston: Allyn and Bacon.

Sciarra, D.T. (1999). Intrafamilial separations in the immigrant family: Implications for cross-cultural counseling. *Journal of Multicultural Counseling and Development, 27,* 31–41.

Sciarra, D.T., & Ponterotto, J.G. (1993). Counseling the Hispanic bilingual family: Challenges to the therapeutic process. *Psychotherapy, 28,* 473–479.

Sluzki, C.E. (1979). Migration and family conflict. *Family Process, 18,* 379–390.

Szapocznik, J., & Kurtines, W.M. (1993). Family psychology and cultural diversity. *American Psychologist, 48,* 400–407.

Szapocznik, J., Rio, A., Perez-Vidal, A., Kurtines, W., Hervis, O., & Santisteban, D. (1986). Bicultural effectiveness training (BET): An experimental test of an intervention modality for families experiencing intergenerational/intercultural conflict. *Hispanic Journal of Behavioral Sciences, 8,* 303–330.

Szapocznik, J., Santisteban, D., Kurtines, W., Perez-Vidal, A., & Hervis, O. (1984). Bicultural effectiveness training: Treatment for enchancing intercultural adjustment in Cuban American families. *Hispanic Journal of Behavioral Sciences, 6,* 317–344.

CHAPTER 7

—⟨⟩⟨⟩⟨⟩—

MULTICULTURAL CONSULTATION IN ORGANIZATIONS

Sue (1995) raised the issue of whether counselors should be involved in the arena of organizational consultation and development. Since the task interfaces with the business sector, is it not better left to MBAs and industrial/organizational psychologists? The answer would be yes if the understanding is that organizational development and consultation only deals with the technical dimension. However, this is not so, and this book supports a *sociotechnical* approach to organizations—which places equal emphasis on both the human relatedness (socio) dimension of work as well as the technical. The importance of considering people and their personalities, the dynamics of individuals in groups, and the dynamics of intergroup relations can and should be the purview of the counselor. Furthermore, with ever-increasing diversity in the workplace, counselors have a wonderful opportunity to combine principles of interpersonal behavior with those of second-culture acquisition and cultural identity development and to make a significant contribution to organizations at times paralyzed in dealing with such diversity.

As has been the case throughout, the chapter begins with some fundamental concepts in organizational development, followed by an application of multicultural constructs, and ends with two case examples. The latter part of this book has evolved from examinations of the dyad in individual counseling, to the interpersonal in group counseling, to the family system. In considering organizations, a step to another level is taken by examining the interrelatedness of various systems.

THE NATURE OF ORGANIZATIONS

Open Systems Theory

An open system is defined as one that takes in something from the outside, transforms it, and puts out a product. Intake, transformation or conversion, and output are the three defining moments of an open system (Miller & Rice, 1967). Open systems are a part of our everyday living. The human body is an open system, as are our educational institutions—which take in students, educate them, and output them with skills for a particular path in life. A manufacturing company inputs raw materials and converts them into products to be purchased by the consumer. Complex systems have various activities to complete the process of input, transformation, and output, and these activities are interrelated. A simple example, again, is the manufacturing company that will have a purchasing department (those responsible for procuring the material—input), the personnel department (charged with recruiting and training those who will transform what is purchased), and a sales department responsible for having the output consumed. There may also be a quality control department responsible for ensuring that production meets certain requirements. Each of these activities involves different groups of people working interdependently. Therefore, consultation to organizations requires not only a working knowledge of the fundamentals of open systems but a theory of human behavior (Miller & Rice, 1967). A consultant must not only understand something about the input, transformation, and output of an organization but must also examine how the different groups within an organization are relating across boundaries.

For a group to have a defined identity, it must have a boundary around it; however, these boundaries, as we saw in the chapter on families, will differ in their degree of rigidity or diffuseness. The uniqueness of organizations is that they must have boundaries around their distinct activity groups for purposes of autonomy and identity, but at the same time these groups need to speak with one another. Sales people ought not influence the production process nor vice versa, yet sales and production must relate to one another for the organization to be healthy. This is usually done through representation by one or more members of the activity group who meet on a regular basis. These representatives form another group whose activity is representation, communication, and usually decision making. One begins to see how intergroup relatedness and interaction become the heart of organizational consultation, as difficulties in this arena can cause major problems and even disaster for an organization. Thus, it is important to look more closely at the dynamics of intergroup relations.

Intergroup Perspective in Organizations

The well-known Hawthorne studies (see Roethlisberger & Dickson, 1939) conducted at the Western Electric plant in Chicago in the early 1930s began with the goal of studying the effects of environmental variables, such as lighting and noise, upon worker productivity. The researchers found that whether variables were manipulated positively or negatively, worker productivity increased. The conclusion of the studies became known as the "Hawthorne Effect," signifying that the work group's special status of being research participants was responsible for greater productivity. The implication of the Hawthorne studies is that how work groups are treated will more significantly affect their level of productivity than will the "technical" aspects of the organization. This research, done over 60 years ago, fortuitously paved the way for the study of intergroup relations in organizations.

Identity Groups Versus Organizational Groups. In the chapter on groups, we saw how both intrapsychic and interpersonal forces powerfully influence the life of a group through transference and protective identifications. Analogously, when studying intergroup relations (the relations among different work groups in an organization), one must examine group-level forces and tranferences. Alderfer (1986) lists the following as forces affecting intergroup behavior: group boundaries, power differences, affective patterns, cognitive formations, and leadership behavior. These forces apply to the two classes of groups which exist in every organization: identity groups based on race, ethnicity, gender, family (especially if it's a family-run business), age, and so forth; and organizational groups based on the division of labor and hierarchy of authority whereby the members share common organizational positions (Alderfer, 1986). Identity groups and organizational groups tend to be highly related. For example, in the United States, top management positions are held for the most part by middle-aged, White males. The potential for serious conflict in an organization exists when group members perceive the allocation of, or access to, resources as based on race or ethnicity. In more general terms, if the assignment to organizational groups is a function of identity group, the organization is guilty of institutional discrimination.

Parallel Process. This is an important concept in studying intergroup relations and for dealing with "processes whereby two or more human systems in relationship to one another seem to infect and become infected by one another" (Alderfer, 1986, p. 210). A simple example would be a counselor and a supervisor who replicate in their relationship the dynamics present in the relationship between the client and the counselor. In organizations, parallel process exists on an intergroup level in a situation in which the dynamics of one work group will be replicated (paralleled) in another work group, resulting in similar affect, behavior, and cognition. Leaders of different work groups who meet on a regular basis have a certain dynamic, which then becomes replicated in their different work groups. If, for example, this group of leaders deals with the anxiety of top management through denial of any existing problems, then their work groups will also function under a similar dynamic. Organizations that function this way can limp forward through minor cover-ups—until it's too late, and the organization finds itself on the brink of disaster.

Though a later section will deal completely with organizational diagnosis, it is worth mentioning here that one of the most important tasks of the consultant is to analyze the parallel process that exists on the intergroup level in an organization. What is the fundamental process that suffuses the different groups in this particular workplace? Parallel process need not be destructive; it can also be constructive. However, when an organization recruits a consultant for a problem situation, the working goal is the discovery of a parallel process that is deleterious to the productivity of the organization. If work groups are able to step back periodically from the task at hand and examine the process taking place in their own groups, such awareness can interrupt a destructive parallel process infecting an organization. A skilled consultant can help an organization develop this kind of awareness. Dysfunctional work groups generally suffer from one of two extremes. They focus only on the tasks at hand with no capacity for examining the human side (i.e., the process of their interaction), or they focus too much on the process and lose sight of the group's primary task.

Organizations as Mechanisms of Defense. Elliot Jaques (1955), renowned consultant to organizations, understood the basic nature of a social system as a defense against anxiety. Social systems or structures arise to calm the anxiety associated with releasing forbidden impulses and to direct one's energy into socially acceptable channels. The loss of work is traumatic for most individuals. On the other hand, how many of us have avoided difficult situations by taking refuge in work?

The organization of work is a social system, and for Jaques a most important question for the consultant is: How is the organization being used by its members to deal with their anxiety? Employing a psychoanalytical perspective, Jaques divides this anxiety into two basic types: paranoid and depressive. Paranoid anxiety creates a social system based on fear, lack of trust, and a "we versus them" mentality (between workers and management, for example). It is a social system that revolves around the fear of a common enemy. Depressive anxiety, on the other hand, creates a system that needs a "fall person" or a scapegoat. It's an organization that seeks to blame by dividing the members into a good majority and bad minority. The chapter on groups highlighted the significant role played by the management of anxiety among group members. With organizations, the consultant must examine this same phenomenon, but more on the intergroup level. The consultant's best-laid plans can go to waste for failure to take into account how the institution is being used by its members to deal with their anxiety. For example, the consultant's first instinct might be to counteract scapegoating in the organization—without realizing that the social system survives around this dynamic. The consultant would fare better by analyzing first the common anxieties in the workplace and the not-so-conscious collusions underlying various relationships in the organization.

ORGANIZATIONAL ROLE THEORY

The sociotechnical approach to organizations requires a constant attempt to optimize both the social and technical systems. Every prospective employer is asking three questions about applicants: Can they do the job?; Will they do the job?; and Will they fit in? (Heather Dawson, personal communication, May 1995). The first question has to do with technical capability, the second with motivation, and the third with the match between the individual's personality and the organization's social system. It is this last aspect of the work environment that is developed here.

The sociotechnical approach in studying the human relations dimension of an organization ought not to neglect the influence of personality upon the social structure. Unlike the strict approach of sociologists, the counselors/consultants, because of their special training, are equipped to examine both the psychological determinants within an individual and their "fit" with the social system. Though the system is more powerful than any one individual, a common experience in the workplace is the inordinate influence of one personality, be it an asset or a liability.

Levinson (1959) talked about role development and performance within an organization as the confluence of two forces: the role demands of the organization and determinants within individuals (personality characteristics). Organizational role demands are divided into formal and informal. Formal role demands include official norms and contract descriptions issued by the administration, while informal demands include input by various individuals or groups as to how they think the role ought to be performed. Confronted with the formal and informal norms of the organizational role, individuals must effectuate their own particular mode of adaptation, depending on their own values, goals, and ego identity. For example, there exists a strong connection between family role and organizational role (Singer & Shapiro, 1989). Only after examining one's family role can individuals become aware of their organizational role and fully assume the responsibility for such a role and maintain its boundaries.

Previously discussed was the importance of boundary making in an organization, among different groups within the organization, and between the organization and the outside world. Equally important is the maintenance of the boundary around one's role. Some may argue that such boundary making is limiting and diminishes the creative capacity of a worker. However, the opposite is true. Only by staying in one's role, knowing and understanding one's place in the organization, and feeling reconciled with that place can an individual effectively relate to others in the organization. Staying in one's role is a way to bind the anxiety and impulses of the inner self (Schachtel, 1990). Leaving one's role crosses a boundary from the institutional to the noninstitutional, which can lead to serious problems in the workplace.

Let's take as a simple example the supervisors who show appreciation to their workers by inviting them to lunch or dinner every so often. This socialization experience is still within the role of the supervisor (showing appreciation) and therefore not harmful. On the other hand, the supervisors who create an expectation that their workers are to accompany them for drinks after work (the assumption being they need someone to drink with) does violate role boundaries, creates confusion, and actually exacerbates anxiety because of role deinstitutionalization. The differences between these two scenarios are fundamental and significant. In the first, coworkers are appreciated for who they are; in the second, they are appreciated for gratifying the supervisor's social needs. Coming out of one's role allows other traits of the personality structure to take over—aspects that are less capable of managing destructive impulses. Hirschhorn (1988) understood role boundary and management as a proper vehicle for sublimation and rejecting fantasies of omnipotence.

In conclusion, organizational consultants must become cognizant of the formal and informal structures of an organization and how these determine role definition. Furthermore, they must become aware of how role boundaries are maintained or not maintained within the organization, on both the personal and intergroup level. Proper role management is crucial to the human relations dimension of the workplace, and its violation can lead to the most deleterious forms of exploitation and harassment.

LEADERSHIP AND AUTHORITY IN ORGANIZATIONS

> The main objective of an organization is not to satisfy the human needs of its members but to carry out a task. One objective of intelligent leadership is to permit the gratification of human needs in carrying out that task. (Kernberg, 1985)

When speaking about leadership, the old nature versus nurture argument rears its head. Are good leaders born or made? Bad leadership is the psychological result of using others as repositories for the despised and mangled parts of ourselves that have been split off and projected onto others (Gould, 1989). Splitting and projection were discussed earlier as a psychological mechanism for understanding interpersonal behavior in group counseling. It is also a useful concept in understanding group relations in an organization—and most especially, the relationship between leaders and their workers. For example, authoritarian leadership is the result of projecting onto others (usually marginal groups) one's own unacceptable impulses and behaviors, with the resulting attitude that they must be controlled and carefully watched (Adorno, Frenkel-Brunswick, Levinson, & Sonford, 1950). However, in an organization, the character structure alone of a particular authority figure is not sufficient to explain the type of authority being exercised. It may also stem from features of the organizational structure (Kernberg, 1985). A strong hierarchical organizational structure with authority centralized in one or a few members most likely will nurture a more authoritarian form of leadership, as opposed to a flatter structure where authority is more evenly distributed.

Kernberg (1985) talked about problems in leadership along the lines of four personality types: schizoid, obsessive, paranoid, and narcissistic. These can apply both to an individual authority figure as well as to authority in the organization as a whole. Though traits of one type will dominate in all leaders, problems in leadership result from regression along these lines of personality, resulting in severe splitting and projection. Good leaders are able to reign in these regressive pulls and balance the positive aspects of each to create proper boundaries between themselves and their staff, pay appropriate attention to the actual running of the organization, maintain a modest amount of watchfulness and concern for discontent in the organization, and be unoffensively proud and accepting of their leadership role. Whenever these positive characteristics become unboundedly exaggerated, leadership regression takes over along the lines of the four personality types stated by Kernberg and described below.

Schizoid. These are the leaders who isolate themselves most of all emotionally and frustrate the workers' needs for warmth, support, and understanding.

Obsessive. These are very efficient leaders who reinforce the bureaucratic aspects at the expense of sacrificing creativity among members. They can be sadistic, forcing workers to submit to the rules of the organization and thus interfering with any kind of personal creativity.

Paranoid. If this problem type is severe, any kind of discussion or minor opposition will be interpreted by these leaders as a hidden attack, dangerous and rebellious. Therefore, their reaction is to suppress and control the "opposition," which results in staff becoming afraid—fear in the leader breeds fear in the staff. It is a form of leadership that leads to a fight/flight mentality. Workers feel they must either flee or fight back, usually through the emergence of another leader. Paranoid leadership also creates an in-group (a small number of people who are close to the leader) and a large out-group (those who cannot be trusted and must be controlled).

Narcissistic. This is perhaps the most serious form of regression in leaders. Narcissistic leaders have a strong need for power and prestige and therefore easily can rise to leadership positions. They thrive on the submission and admiration of staff, increase staff's dependency, and prefer to be surrounded by "yes-men." There is little recognition for the success of others as the narcissistic leader is very jealous and easily threatened.

Part of the consultant's diagnosis must include the kind of leadership present in an organization, the qualities of the leaders and their regressive pulls, and whether these are a problem for the organization. If they are a problem, the question arises as to whether the leader can be helped to change or should be helped to leave (Kernberg, 1985). Moreover, a way to offset the deleterious effects of any one leader is to promote a more participatory management style within the organization.

The Kernberg typology is only one way among many that a counselor/consultant can analyze the form of leadership present in the organization. The more important issue is to take very seriously the kind of leadership that is identified and its effect upon members of the organization.

ORGANIZATIONAL DIAGNOSIS

The consultant's first task, much like that of the counselor in other settings, is to understand the cause of the organization's problems. As does the individual counselee, the organization expresses its problems via a symptom(s)—the means by which it asks for help and for a different form of understanding (Bain, 1981). The symptom generally hides something deeper and acts as a defense against the anxiety of having to face the real causes of the organization's problems (Gilmore & Krantz, 1985). Thus, the purpose of organizational diagnosis is to produce a new level of awareness within the system, which in turn will result in cultural and structural changes (Bartee & Cheyunski, 1977). The sociotechnical approach of organizational development requires the discovery of these out-of-awareness dynamics.

Alderfer (1980) divides the organizational diagnosis into three phases: entry, data collection, and feedback.

Entry

How the consultant enters an organization is crucial, as many consultations fail at entry (Berg, 1977). Unless the consultant is dealing at entry with the true leader(s) and powerbroker(s) of the organization, the consultation will have little, if any, significant impact. The consultant, in order to ensure successful entry, must first assess the boundaries of the organization along a continuum of overboundedness and underboundedness.

Overbounded Organizations. According to Alderfer (1976), these organizations have highly impermeable boundaries, creating a system that is rigid and overcontrolled. Authority is well-defined and constrains initiatives from below, withholds needed information, and specifies clearly the rules; though meetings take place, they do so only to enhance the self-interest of the communicator. The consultant entering this kind of organization will have little problem discovering who the real leaders are but will experience tremendous difficulty in permeating the organization's boundaries and accessing valuable information and data about the organization.

Underbounded Organizations. In these organizations, authority, assignments, and rules are not clear. Meetings for the most part do not take place, and the organization has difficulty harnessing the energy of its workers. Upon entry, the consultant will have easy access to people and information; however, the challenge is discovering the relevant leaders. Here, the consultant runs the risk of joining initially with members of the organization whose impact is minimal.

Consultants must know upon entry whether they are facing an overbounded or underbounded system because it will affect their mode of proceeding. For example, in the overbounded system, the consultant must work with the clearly designated leader of the organization, build a strong rapport first, and then gradually gain access to sources of information. On the other hand, in the underbounded organization, the consultant's first task is to discover the real leadership in the organization by working with people and information that are readily available.

Data Collection

Traditional methods used in gathering data for an organization have included surveys, formal/structured interviews, and participant observation. While these methods continue to be valuable ways of gathering information, the counselor's unique training allows for another form of data collection, equally valid yet more dynamic: the use of feelings. The consultant is just as much an object of the leader's projective identification as are the workers within the organization. More often than not, the manager of an organization will deny responsibility for a situation and project that responsibility onto others, the consultant being no exception (Gilmore & Krantz, 1985). The consultant is invited to collude in the same projective identification process that has shaped the organization, made it incapable of dealing with its problems, and now requires it to call in an outside consultant. "The client conveys his picture to the consultant including those aspects of the problem which the client is denying to himself" (Bain, 1981, as cited in Gilmore & Krantz, 1985, p. 1164). Thus, how consultants are made to *feel* about the problem and about their role in helping with the problem becomes data for the assessment (Gilmore & Krantz, 1985). Just as in individual counseling where counselors use their affective awareness to gain greater understanding of clients, so too consultants use such awareness to deepen understanding of the organization. For example, if the consultant feels a pull to overfunction, the invitation is to collude in the denial of responsibility that is most likely pervasive within the organization. The consultant who enacts the role of overfunctioner colludes and begins to act less like a consultant and more like a member of the organization. What is the client pulling for? What dysfunctional process am I being invited to collude in? These are extremely important diagnostic questions that often are answered not through intellectual but affective means. This is where counselors' training interfaces nicely with organizational consultation and assessment.

Weisbord (1976) listed the following six areas that the consultant needs to assess: purpose, structure, relationships, rewards, leadership, and helpful mechanisms. Leadership was dealt with in a previous section; therefore, below is an examination of Weisbord's other areas of assessment.

Purpose. The consultant clearly must understand the formal purpose of the organization, its reason for being, or its primary task as formally stated. This can usually be found in company charters or mission statements. In a next step, the consultant must assess the degree of congruency between what the organization says it does and what people within the organization actually do. If these are incongruent, there is a problem.

Structure. The consultant must examine both the formal and informal structures of the organization that reveal how the work is divided. The formal structure is usually gleaned from an organizational chart, but the informal structure must be discovered through observation and interviews to assess the actual hierarchy and work distribution in the organization. Once again, the consultant assesses the fit between these two structures.

Relationships. An examination of the organization's kind and degree of conflict between people, or between units, or between people and technology is crucial to a proper assessment. Many organizations will have official policies regarding the resolution of conflicts, but many are dealt with in more informal ways. The consultant assesses the congruency between the two and looks carefully at whether the informal structure for dealing with conflict favors some over others.

Rewards. How are people rewarded in the organization—both formally and informally? Does the reward system favor some members over others? Some tasks over others? The consultant must also assess the degree to which the members *feel* rewarded and how congruent this is with actual rewards they receive.

Helpful Mechanisms. This is a general category used to assess the technology, support systems, and management of information in the organization. What systems are in place to help members perform their jobs better and how they function in practice is the last important area for the consultant to assess.

In general, the consultant is attempting to assess how big a gap exists between the formal and informal systems in each of these areas (Weisbord, 1976). The greater the discrepancy between what the organization says officially and what actually takes place, the greater the potential conflict and dissatisfaction among its members. In discussing organizational intervention, the next section deals with the discrepancy between what is and what ought to be.

Feedback

After data collection is completed, the consultant's next step is to provide feedback to the organization. This is a crucial step in the consultation process as it can mark either the end of the consultation or the beginning of a new phase, should the client decide that the organization must change. Ideally, feedback should be given to all members of the organization, and this can be done in different-sized groups organized by the function that members provide for the organization. Superiors and subordinates should be present at the same time.

During feedback meetings, defenses are high on the part of both the client and the consultant. The client fears hearing things that are wrong with the organization, while the consultant fears being wrong about the organization. Alderfer (1976) suggested that the consultant provide feedback in the form of tentative hypotheses, allowing for the client's reaction to such formulations. In this fashion, the provision of feedback becomes more of a collaborative endeavor rather than the diagnostician's proclamation of absolute truth. If resistance is strong on the part of the client, it signals one of two things: Either the organization is very defensive and not ready to change or the diagnosis is inadequate or wrong (Alderfer, 1976).

In the best-case scenario, the collaborative form of the feedback session(s) will lessen the client's resistance to an accurate diagnosis. If such is the case, the consultant may well be invited to continue the consultation by helping the organization manage change.

CONSULTANT'S ROLE IN MANAGING CHANGE

Consulting is a "function of providing help on the content, process, structure of a task or series of tasks where the consultant is not actually responsible for doing the task itself but is helping those who are" (Beckhard, 1969, p. 93). This is a good working definition of consultation for which there are various models.

Models of Consultation

Schein (1969, 1978) has proposed three basic models of consultation.

Purchase of Expertise Model. In this model, the consultant is viewed as an expert hired to solve a problem that the organization has diagnosed and communicated to the consultant. After such communication has taken place, the responsibility for solving the problem rests with the consultant's expertise. In this model, the success of the consultation is dependent upon the accuracy of the diagnosis made by the organization (Rockwood, 1993).

Doctor-Patient Model. In this model, the consultant is charged with diagnosing the problem and prescribing a solution. The organization's responsibility is to provide sufficient and necessary data enabling the consultant to make a proper diagnosis (Rockwood, 1993).

Process Consultation Model. In this model, the focus is less on the content of the problem and more on how problems are solved (Rockwood, 1993). Process consultation involves the client throughout the entire process of diagnosis, generation of solutions, and implementation of interventions. Unlike the previous two models, process consultation emphasizes a collaborative relationship between consultant and client.

All three models can be appropriate for a given consultation. One of the consultant's first tasks is to determine the most appropriate role given the nature of the organization. Role management on the part of the consultant is one of the key ingredients to a successful consultation.

Redefinition of Boundaries

As mentioned earlier, organizations with problems in human relations have boundary issues. By maintaining a proper boundary around their own role, the consultants can help the organization redefine its own boundaries. Since boundaries have to do with control and power, any reorganization will set off concerns and maneuvering for power. Yet, the dilemma of any organization is to maintain a sense of both identity and autonomy (by tightening the boundary) and the necessary interdependence and integration (by loosening the boundary) (Schneider, 1991). Once consultants have clarified the primary task and boundaries of the organization, they must ask: To what degree are the organizational boundaries helping or hurting the accomplishment of the primary task? Are the boundaries overly rigid and defined, causing fragmentation? Or insufficient, causing overlap and redundancy? The consultant's task is to identify the key links and facilitate the renegotiation of boundaries in one direction or the other, both within the organization and between the organization and the outside world.

Managing the Transition

Working with the key leadership of the organization, the consultant must "develop and communicate a clear image of the future" (Nadler, 1981). As in individual counseling, clearly stated and defined goals are crucial for establishing leverage in the consultation. A clear understanding and acceptance of the desired state of the organization and a strong commitment by key leadership to that desired state is a critical ingredient for the success of any consultation.

Another important arrangement for managing change in the organization is for the consultant to work closely with a "transition manager," who may or may not be the chief executive but who is in charge of implementing changes in the organization and receiving feedback about such changes. Often, a manager may assume that a certain change is taking place only to find out later that nothing was done (Nadler, 1981). Any organization undergoing significant reorganization needs to have viable feedback mechanisms to avoid denial on the part of the managerial staff as to the challenges and difficulties in implementing change. The consultant also needs to facilitate open communication between the transition manager and lower-level management.

Resistance and Motivation to Change

As in other forms of counseling, resistance to change within an organization can be pervasive and powerful because it challenges one's need for stability and security. Reorganization sets off concerns for power and control and a search for hidden motives in the leadership. The consultant must be ready to facilitate dealing with such resistance.

Nadler (1981) articulates four action steps that serve to increase motivation to change and reduce resistance: (1) identify and surface dissatisfaction with the current state, since dissatisfied members will be more motivated to change; (2) build in as much participation as possible in the changes from all levels of the organization; (3) build in a reward system for behaviors consistent with the transition and future states of the organization; and (4) give time and opportunity for members of the organization to deal emotionally with the changes. Change implies loss, and workers should be given the opportunity to mourn their loss. Talk of the "good old days" should be allowed, even encouraged, and not seen necessarily as opposition.

In conclusion, organizational consultation/development is intricate and challenging. If counselors/consultants manage their role properly and focus on the human-relatedness dimension of the organization, a significant contribution can be made by the counseling profession to contemporary organizations. Furthermore, when one considers how diversity in the workplace creates more challenges for human relations, the potential contribution of the multiculturally skilled counselor is even greater. The following section deals with some specific issues in working with cultural diversity in organizations.

MULTICULTURAL ORGANIZATIONAL CONSULTATION

Because of its high priority on the human relations factor of organizational development, the sociotechnical approach can be utilized to examine how cultural differences are managed within an organization. As occurs in a multicultural society, an organization's degree of multiculturalism can be measured by how it deals with cultural diversity.

The importance of dealing with issues of diversity in the workplace cannot be overemphasized. White Eurocentric organizational leaders rarely exhibit an informed awareness of racial and ethnic diversity. The majority appear to be at the contact stage, oblivious to issues of race and other forms of cultural diversity and content with the belief that they "treat all people the same"—an attitude that is dismissive of cultural diversity. All people are *not* to be treated the same, because they bring diverse values, strengths, learning styles, forms of interaction, and emotional involvement. Treating all people the same in the organizational world usually means expecting them to conform to a White Eurocentric way of performing. A friend who works at one of the major communications conglomerates recently related how their Asian employees are constantly passed over for higher managerial positions because they are not seen as aggressive enough! According to Sue (1995), if organizations increase their awareness of and value for diversity, they will be in a much better position not only to deal with conflicts arising from such diversity but also to use its potential richness for increasing productivity. Organizational leadership that facilitates employees working together by encouraging them not to overlook their cultural differences but to productively utilize them will, in the long run, enjoy a more successful operation.

The Multicultural Organization

Jackson and Holvino (1988) defined a multicultural organization as having the following four characteristics: It (1) adequately and appropriately reflects the contributions and interests of diverse cultural groups in all dimensions of the open system (input, transformation, and output); (2) is committed to eliminating all forms of social oppression within its boundary; (3) includes members of diverse cultural and social groups as full participants in the decision-making process; and (4) goes beyond the organizational boundaries in eliminating social oppression and heightening sensitivity to cultural diversity.

Before an organization becomes truly multicultural, it passes through various stages of development, which Jackson and Holvino (1988) have hypothesized as six:

The Exclusionary Organization. Here, the organization systematically excludes nondominant groups from any significant participation. The goal is the maintenance of one particular cultural group in power and control.

The Club. This organization allows members from different cultural groups to participate as long as they buy into the modus operandi of the dominant group. The unique cultural contributions brought by the different members must be left at the "club" door.

The Compliance Organization. This organization is concerned with appearing politically correct and therefore provides access to women and minorities—but without disturbing the mission, structure, or culture of the organization as defined by the dominant group. "Token" minorities are admitted to management positions as an attempt to eliminate some of the club's discrimination but must not rock the boat and are expected to be "team" players—promoters of the status quo.

The Affirmative Action Organization. Committed to reducing discrimination, this organization supports the hiring and promotion of more than just a few minorities and attempts to ensure their success by providing special supports and working actively with nonminority members to think and behave in a nonoppressive manner. Nevertheless, this is an organization whose culture (norms, practices, and so forth) is still defined by the dominant group.

The Redefining Organization. Not content with being just antiracist or antisexist, this organization seeks to distribute power among all of the diverse groups and calls into question its prevailing cultural perspective. This organization begins to understand, appreciate, and utilize the benefits of a multicultural workforce.

The Multicultural Organization. The final stage of development, this organization conforms to the principles outlined above for a true multicultural organization. The organization is proactively committed to reducing cultural oppression both within and without, and it reflects equally the contributions of a diverse workforce throughout its operations.

Similar to racial/cultural identity models previously discussed, the foregoing model for organizations moves from simple nonawareness and/or exclusionary position regarding cultural differences to an all-inclusive appreciation for the potential rich contribution of cultural diversity within the workplace. Thus, embarking on multicultural organizational consultation would require as a first diagnostic question: At what stage of multicultural development is this organization?

Based on the answer to this question, the multicultural consultant will proceed accordingly. For example, earlier stages of multicultural development would require efforts aimed more at individuals or a specific group viewed as responsible for maintaining and promoting a monocultural organization. As increased sensitivity to cultural diversity becomes the goal, workshops and training seminars are offered, along with support groups for the oppressed within the organization. In the latter stages of multicultural development, interventions are more systemwide, and the emphasis is upon team building and skills for managing differences (Jackson & Holvino, 1988). At these levels of development, the consultant facilitates an environment in which the different work groups in an organization can deal openly with their differences, especially those that evolve out of their different cultural backgrounds. In the multicultural organization, work group members are able to "process" their differences with both an awareness and a comfort that such differences are culturally based. The consultant can develop workshops and seminars using the constructs of second-culture acquisition and cultural identity development to facilitate discussion and growth around cultural differences.

Women and Minorities in Management

Perhaps nothing in the last 10 years has stimulated more research and controversy in the workplace than the changing face of American management as many corporations have sought to promote both women and minorities. In the 1980s, approximately a third of management positions were filled by women as compared to 19% in 1972 (Hymowitz & Schellhardt, 1986), yet only 1.7% of corporate officerships in the Fortune 500 were held by women (Von Glinow & Krzyczkowska-Mercer as cited in Morrison & Von Glinow, 1990). Statistics seem to indicate that although women are promoted to management positions more than before, there is a point in the management hierarchy beyond which they rarely pass. A similar phenomenon exists for racial minorities. In 1979, a survey by the major research firm of Korn/Ferry International of 1,708 senior executives showed three Blacks, two Asians, and two Hispanics. In 1985, a similar survey showed four Blacks, six Asians, and three Hispanics. Explanations for this lack of managerial progress have included deficiency theory—women and minorities are simply inappropriate as managers; discrimination theory—organizations are basically exclusionary, resulting in bias on the part of the dominant group; and systemic theory—that the identity groups of women and minorities and the stereotypes associated with them do not change in spite of a change in their organizational groups (Morrison & Von Glinow, 1990).

As mentioned earlier, Alderfer (1986) made an important distinction between identity groups and organizational groups—a distinction that can play itself out in the case of women in management. Our society stereotypically has associated dominance and independence with the masculine, and submissiveness, passivity, and nurturance with the feminine. Within the family system, these roles have been delineated along the lines of external and internal boundaries. Traditionally, males have been charged with managing the external boundary between the family and the outside world, with providing money and protecting the family from harmful, outside forces. Females traditionally have been charged with managing the internal boundary, with people and events internal to the family. An organization must negotiate carefully both its external and internal boundaries. The higher one moves along the organizational hierarchy, the greater the responsibility for managing the external boundary. Lower-level management positions are usually confined to managing events and interpersonal relations internal to the organization, whereas higher-level management and most all CEOs deal with their organizations' relationships to the outside world. Thus, one begins to see how traditional sex-linked roles make it difficult for women to rise to CEO status of an organization. Based on role theory, there is a certain incongruity between the identity role and the organizational role, "between the need of the group to have its leader protect the external boundary and the traditional concept of a woman protected by a powerful male and vulnerable to rape and seduction" (Bayes & Newton, 1978, p. 11). This could explain why women whose work involves the internal boundary of an organization rise to management positions but have a much more difficult time rising to positions where the primary responsibility is managing the external boundary.

Finally, the multicultural organizational consultant must be keenly aware of gender issues in the workplace inasmuch as deeply ingrained cultural stereotypes may be preventing the organization from tapping the potential resources of women and minorities in management positions. The multiculturally skilled consultant should facilitate an organization's dealing with issues of gender and race and, as counselors, enjoy the added advantage of interpreting such issues through the lens of psychological projections, the result of cultural stereotypes.

CASE EXAMPLE 1

I remember vividly the day Louis called me. It was cold, rainy, and I had the flu. Louis was the general manager of a relatively small electronic component company located in the Northeast, which I will call Slick Electronics. Louis said he received my name from a manager at a sister company (Slick was owned by a nationally known company with various holdings) who said I might be able to help. When I asked what seemed to be the problem, Louis said that some of his managers were not performing, and this was hurting the company. We agreed to meet and talk further about the problem.

Just from the phone conversation, I didn't like Louis. He came across as pompous, and from his tone I felt somewhat diminished in the conversation. Whether my sickly state had something to do with this, I don't know. However, my hypothesis was that Louis himself was in trouble with the parent company, and I suspected that it was "strongly recommended" he get some outside help. Although Louis blamed his managers for the company's problems, I had to wonder if his position was vulnerable with higher-ups at the parent company.

Background Information

From my first meeting with Louis and a tour of the plant, I learned the following about the company. Slick made capacitors, which were sold to high-tech electronic companies. These capacitors were inserted on printed circuit boards for use in just about every industry. Slick was a classic open system. They imported raw materials of ceramic powder, binder, and solvents that were then mixed and cast into sheets. These sheets underwent "green processing," where they were punched, printed, and laminated, after which they were fired and electrically tested. This final capacitor underwent quality control checks and was then shipped with a distribution of 40% to Asia, 45% to North America, and 15% to Europe. It was quite an easy operation to grasp, and I was impressed by the smooth running of the manufacturing process.

The problem was that Slick had been losing money for almost two years. Though they faced stiff competition from Japanese capacitor companies, Slick had previously found its niche in the market in order to make itself profitable. Recently sales had plummeted, even though the companies to which Slick had traditionally sold were doing well. It seemed they were going elsewhere for their capacitors. Slick had undergone a series of significant layoffs, and this had cut deeply into the morale of the workers without solving the problem.

Louis had been the general manager for almost two years, succeeding Wayne, who had been forced out of the organization by corporate management. Wayne had had a long-standing affair with Phyllis, who quickly rose in the organization from working in personnel to production manager. Wayne's wife sued him, which precipitated a long and ugly divorce settlement; the marriage of Wayne and Phyllis ensued. Shortly thereafter, the brass of the parent company forced Phyllis, and then Wayne, out of the organization. Louis, as Wayne's replacement, came as a surprise to many at Slick. He had not been with the organization very long and had no managerial experience behind him. He entered the organization as an engineer with a relatively high salary, given the expertise he provided at the time.

Entry

At my first meeting with Louis, he was more charming than over the phone. Part of me felt good about my entry into the organization because Louis was organizationally and formally the leader at Slick. He was the number-one man, and he was contracting me. However, I knew instinctually that I had been forced upon Louis, and that he would resent me for it. Developing a true working alliance with Louis would be an enormous challenge, and I was not hopeful that the consultation would be carried through to its conclusion. I explained to Louis my mode of working, the sociotechnical approach to organization, and the importance of the human-relatedness dimension. Louis readily agreed, saying that he felt part of the problem was relational issues among his managers. When I asked for anyone or anything in particular, Louis mentioned especially the one female manager, Cindy, in charge of manufacturing engineering. However, Louis qualified that Cindy had "come around" as of late. My curiosity was piqued, and I looked forward to meeting and speaking with Cindy, whose husband also worked for Slick and was the product manager in sales.

I explained to Louis that it was important for me to speak with as many representatives from all levels and sectors of the organization as possible. Louis questioned this, saying he felt the problem was only with the managers. While I agreed as to the importance of speaking with all of the managers, I explained to Louis that problems reverberate. Behind my insistence was the concept of parallel process, and I wanted to see how problems at the top were reflected at the bottom. I told Louis that after this "data collection" I would present him with a "diagnosis" that would conclude the first part of the consultancy. We then could negotiate its continuation.

Finally, I asked Louis to present me formally by memo to the organization and suggested that we work together on this memo. I wanted him to provide the reason for the consultancy, encourage employees to speak freely, and guarantee the confidentiality of their statements. Louis balked at the request for confidentiality (as I thought he would) because I was asking him to take ownership of the consultation and draw a boundary between himself and the staff. I readily dismissed his objection—that it would be good for him to know those who were displeased—by explaining that without the guarantee of confidentiality I could in no way access genuine and legitimate information. Louis finally agreed, but I knew that our first meeting ended with his liking me even less.

Data Collection

After Louis, I decided to interview all six managers and several of the line supervisors and workers. Since Slick was small, I felt confident that through these semistructured interviews, I would be able to access enough information to offer an informed diagnosis. What follows are the results of my interviews with the different groups and, of course, with Louis himself.

Louis. Having risen to the number-one position in the organization in less than a year, Louis felt that some of his managers were jealous of him, and this might explain what he called their "lack of loyalty." Louis detailed how he tried to cultivate good working relationships with his managers by inviting them to his house and to other social activities when he first took over as general manager. This sent up a red flag for me, and I began to question the boundaries that perhaps Louis violated in order to seduce his staff into liking and accepting him. His insistence on loyalty made me see Louis as having both paranoid and narcissistic traits in his leadership style. I felt the message also was being given to me as a consultant that I, too, must be loyal or else. I had to conclude that this was a dynamic that was present between Louis and his managerial staff. His suspicion of me would complicate the working alliance, so at one point I tried to feed his narcissism by talking about the advantages and disadvantages of being a consultant. The advantage was that I did not work for the organization, but the disadvantage was that I could be dismissed at any time—no questions asked. My intervention at the beginning was to join Louis's need for power and control and hopefully reduce some of his paranoid suspicion of me. I decided not to fight Louis, although the pull was there because I continued to feel diminished in his presence.

I also experienced Louis as very male. He had a strong physical presence, and his office was filled with sporting memorabilia, including a rifle hanging on the wall. It came as little surprise to me that Louis's biggest problem was with his only female manager. I looked forward to my meeting with her and the rest of the managerial staff.

The Managerial Staff. Because of some of the things Louis generated in me (my also needing to be loyal, my wanting to fight him, and my feeling diminished), I decided to meet first with the managers as a group. Both on paper and at first sight, they were an impressive bunch: young, energetic, well-educated engineers who seemed to welcome the presence of a consultant. I knew I would have to resist strongly being seduced and entering into a coalition with them against Louis. It would be easy: They were likeable and Louis was not.

Cindy, the only woman, was immediately noticeable: blond, petite, attractive, articulate, and well educated (she and her husband both had PhDs in ceramic engineering). My immediate reaction to her was: small in stature, big in influence. The managers appeared to be a very cohesive group, saying they worked well together and enjoyed working for Slick. It was a small company but always had managed to find its niche in the market. The boundaries among their different departments seemed quite fluid, as they communicated well and entered one another's turf without being seen as inappropriate. They supported one another's comments in the meeting; they rarely, if ever, interrupted one another; and no one seemed to talk over anybody. They were so cohesive it was kind of frightening. My instincts told me they had met beforehand and prepared for their meeting with me, which reminded me of Louis's complaint that his managers at times would call a private meeting among themselves. By meeting's end, the dynamic between Louis and them appeared fairly clear. They were a group in rebellion against their leader. However, their rebellion was subtle, and I felt they knew quite well Louis's vulnerabilities. They did not respect him and therefore could dismiss him—at least psychologically. His paranoia fueled their cohesiveness, which in turn increased his paranoia. Every group in rebellion is in the process of giving birth to a new leader, and I found myself wondering who this might be. It was difficult for me to tell from that meeting who the designate was, but I was soon to find out.

The Line Staff. My data collection from both line supervisors and workers took the form of chatting informally with them as I walked the floor of the plant. I also had one meeting with several of the line supervisors, and one meeting with a representative group of workers. Frankly, I was impressed with the apparent smooth running of the operation and the interaction between the line and managerial staff. Their biggest concern was the profitability of the organization and potential layoffs. The line staff had not suffered many layoffs, which had taken place primarily among the higher-paid professional staff. Most appeared to be, and said they were, content working for Slick.

I was especially interested in two things: the attitudes of the non-Whites (two supervisors were Black and several workers were Native American) and the line workers' opinion about and relationship with Louis. The first revealed basically a conformity attitude and an assimilationist mode of adaptation to the White power structure. Several of the Native Americans said they preferred White over Black supervisors, which did not surprise me given their conformist attitudes toward cultural identity. In my dealings with Slick, I saw little to change my opinion that it was not a highly developed multicultural organization. I assessed it to be at the club level of development. When asked about the new general manager, the workers revealed some startling and significant data. Many evidenced an attitude of basic indifference toward Louis; some were not even sure who the general manager was; and more than one person thought that Phil, Cindy's husband, was actually in charge of the organization. This sent up yet another red flag, and I had my answer as to who was being born as the new leader of the organization. The fact that it was Cindy's husband made it all the more interesting. Of course, there was some logic to the workers mistaking Phil. As the product manager, Phil spent a great deal of time on the floor of the plant overseeing manufacturing and had great rapport with the workers; he was a very likeable person. Louis, on the other hand, was inclined toward an underbounded relationship with his managerial staff but an overbounded one with the workers. I construed this as part of his narcissism—he was too superior to mess around with workers on the factory floor. With this newfound information, I looked forward even more to my interview with Cindy.

Cindy. Though I met with almost all of the managers individually, Cindy's interview, as expected, proved to be the most interesting. She was quite candid in her opinion of Louis, whom she referred to as a real "jerk," but finally decided she had to "kiss his butt." Cindy resented deeply Louis's treatment of her, and she was keeping a well-documented folder on her interactions with Louis—who she felt was guilty of sexual harassment.

Cindy described the history of the relationship with Louis. When he first took over, she and her husband, along with the other managers, socialized a great deal with him. She recalled a particular evening dinner at Louis's house where they were shown the hot tub and were told the requirement that no clothes were permitted. Later that evening, Louis made an off-handed invitation to enter the hot tub, but it did not materialize. Cindy related other inappropriate incidents involving Louis and said there was gossip at Slick that he wanted to sleep with her. After the so-called "honeymoon" phase with Louis, Cindy, disliking many of the ways Louis was trying to manage the organization, began her outright rebellion. He finally called her to task, demanded her loyalty, and said he could ruin her career if he wanted to. Her rebellion subsided, and she decided to play along. Cindy was not clear as to why she had adopted this position of least resistance, but two things occurred to me. One had to do with her husband possibly being groomed to take over from Louis; second, she knew deep down she ultimately had the upper hand. If she would go to corporate with her list of accusations against Louis, it could be the final nail in his coffin. However, if she was subtly promoting her husband as Louis's successor, the most politically astute position might be to play along for the time being and "kiss Louis's butt." One last item was her repeated requests to go out and visit customers, which Louis had flatly denied. Her responsibilities, which were many and all internal to the organization, included the running of the furnace and supervision of health and safety.

Based on this information, I assessed in terms of cultural identity development that Louis and Cindy had a crossed relationship that exacerbated their problems. Cindy, as a woman in a male-dominated organization, had minority status and was emerging out of dissonance into resistance. Louis, a clear representative of the dominant male culture, was a reintegrated male. As mentioned earlier, crossed relationships have the poorest prognosis for developing into good working alliances.

Diagnosis

Space limitations prevent reporting all of the data. Consultants need not report the data exhaustively but must compose a working diagnosis first for themselves and then for presentation to the leader of the organization, and hopefully to the entire staff. What follows are working ideas about Slick according to some of the categories outlined in the first half of this chapter and that serve as a foundation for a working note that I would present to Louis, thus concluding the first part of the consultation.

Boundaries. Slick had a problem with boundaries at the highest level of management. Louis's predecessor had been forced out of the organization for having an affair and eventually marrying a coworker. When he took over, Louis committed the all-too-frequent mistake of wanting to socialize with his managers in the most intimate way. His managers colluded at first, resulting in a very loose boundary. Eventually, feeling perhaps uncomfortable with that kind of relationship, they redrew a strict boundary between Louis and themselves that increased Louis's anxiety and paranoia, with his consequential accusations of lack of loyalty and the assumption of a more authoritarian stance.

Thus, one recommendation for Slick would be to redraw the boundary between Louis and his managers. They need to reach a middle ground between all being in the hot tub with their clothes off and the "I can ruin your career" stance.

Management of Anxiety. Boundary making and management of anxiety go together. Boundaries, whether they be loose or strict, are designed to manage anxiety within the organization. At present, the managers at Slick are dealing with their anxiety through a fight/flight dynamic (Bion, 1959). In fighting Louis, they give themselves purpose and cohesion. Louis responds in the only way he knows by fighting back and adopting a "stronger than thou" attitude. If this dynamic continues, Louis may well be the loser. The solution would be to move the group out of fight/flight mentality, and this can only be done by coaching, encouraging, and supporting Louis toward a more participatory and collaborative style of management. How possible this is, only time will tell.

Identity Group Versus Organizational Group. Slick is clearly a White-male-dominated organization, and Cindy a prime example of reaching the glass ceiling. She is not allowed to assume any responsibility at the external boundary of the organization. This is reserved for males only, as her desire to go out and meet customers has been flatly denied.

Similar to the traditional female family role, she is charged with the health and safety of the workers and the management of the furnace, a demanding and important task nonetheless. I could not help associate the company's furnace with the family's stove—traditionally overseen by women. Though I do not believe that Slick was actively discriminatory, I did not sense the least bit of sensitivity to gender or to any other issues of diversity. In spite of the fact that engineering is a White-male-dominated profession, Slick has a long way to go before becoming a multicultural organization. However, in this case, the consultant can begin the journey by having Louis examine his relationship with Cindy, along with his refusal to allow her to manage anything on the external boundary. Slick's infantile developmental state regarding issues of diversity may require simply beginning with sensitivity training around gender diversity.

Leadership and Organizational Role. By now, the kind of leadership Louis embodies and the reaction it causes in his managerial staff should be fairly clear. He evidences both narcissistic and paranoid tendencies, and sees himself as a leader who enjoys the reverence, respect, and agreement of his workers. Anything less is construed as a threat to his authority and control. If he senses that the group is giving birth to a new leader in the person of Phil, his paranoia may increase all the more. Of course, one way for Louis to invalidate Phil would be to sleep with his wife, Cindy, something that had been rumored in the organization.

Obviously, the key to a successful consultation in the case of Slick lies in developing a working relationship with Louis. I felt the pull both to suck up to Louis and at the same time to fight him like his managers. Neither would benefit the consultation, and it would be crucial for me to stay in my role as a consultant. Perhaps, I would attempt to have Louis look at his family role and make connections to his organizational role and style of leadership. In many ways, he was being set up as the scapegoat for the organization, and he would have to see that it was in his own self-interest to effectuate a more participatory style of management. I didn't know if this would be possible with Louis, yet I also felt his managers would prove too strong for him in the end. The solution might be a change of leaders. After all, Phil was waiting in the wings, and I didn't think Cindy would be "kissing butt" for very long.

Conclusion

Based on the just-stated ideas, I prepared a working note for presentation first to Louis. I looked forward to our interaction around my assessment. Because of his narcissistic traits, I was careful not to say anything too offensive, yet I had to avoid sugarcoating out of my own fear of Louis. I sent the working note by mail and suggested scheduling a meeting a week later, giving Louis time to digest it. When the time arrived for our meeting, I was very apprehensive, and I knew this did not bode well for me as a consultant. Louis, in some ways, had gotten to me, but I tried as best as possible to remain strong—reminding myself that Louis had the problem, not I.

As I entered Louis's office, he appeared somewhat upbeat. He said he wanted to thank me for what I had done for the organization; however, my services would no longer be needed! Earnings reports had arrived from corporate, and Slick had managed to make money in the last two months! With corporate happy, Louis could dismiss me. He mentioned how he would like to sit and discuss my paper, but he had to run as some top brass from corporate were arriving to discuss Slick's recent success. Whatever money I was owed would be forthcoming. I said I was glad that things had turned around at Slick, and if he ever needed anything not to hesitate contacting me.

Rarely have I felt so invisible, and Louis had managed to provoke an angry reaction in me. Having dismissed me psychologically all along, Louis now relished dismissing me physically. I'm sure my working note wound up in the garbage. I walked away rationalizing that I had made money, but I knew I was hurt. Slick would continue in its current managerial state, and I speculated that, as long as the company was making money, no one—not even Cindy—really cared. The most troubling thing was that in all probability I would never know the solution to my concerns.

CASE EXAMPLE 2

This chapter concludes with a second case example concerning a consultation in a school setting. It is included for two reasons: First, many counselors-in-training will be working in schools; second, issues of cultural diversity within schools are becoming an increasing challenge for administrators, teachers, and students.

When Ted, the superintendent, called, he was quite dismayed over one of his most troubled schools in the district. Last year, the superintendent had been able to replace the school's principal with one of his own choosing. He saw the previous principal as inept and hoped that the new principal would change things rapidly. However, the situation seemed to be getting worse, and this was very troubling to the superintendent. He asked if I would be interested in consulting.

Through other work in this district, I knew something about the school in question. The principal who had been replaced after many years was a Black man, admired and respected by many and seen as inept by a few, namely the superintendent (a White male) and his staff. His replacement was a White woman who had come highly credentialed from another district in this large urban school system. The superintendent mentioned that the new principal was having problems managing the diversity in the school. The student body was 70% Latino and 30% Black; the staff was predominantly non-White—approximately 40% Black, 20% Latino, and 40% White. The school had large bilingual (Spanish) and special education programs and was located in an area of urban blight. The two assistant principals were also new and women: one White, the other Latino.

I was both attracted to and frightened by this consultation. I knew issues of race were at the forefront, as I took the superintendent's remark, "having problems managing diversity," as code for racial tension most likely with staff and possibly parents. Because of my background and interest in issues of racial and cultural diversity, I wanted very much to accept the invitation to consult. However, I also knew that this was a potentially volatile situation and as a White male my effectiveness could be severely compromised.

Entry

The fact that the superintendent called me to consult with one of his principals created a problem of entry. The superintendent was asking for the consult, yet I would not be working with him but the principal. This was not a good situation. Though the superintendent told me on the phone that the principal wanted the consultation (how could she say no to her boss?), I knew I was being imposed upon her, and this would make it almost impossible to establish a working and trusting relationship. I decided to make the superintendent the client—after all he was the one asking for the consult—and suggested that a meeting take place first with him, the principal, and myself. The superintendent balked at this, but I insisted there was no other way. As has been emphasized, consultants must be careful how they enter the organization, and the rule is to go through the door of the person asking for the consult. If not, an issue can arise of passing the buck. The superintendent also had the problem, not just the principal, and it was extremely important for him to be involved in the process.

I had dealt with the superintendent before and knew what to expect. He was a hard-nosed administrator, politically connected and savvy, who had risen through the ranks from being a physical education teacher. I was more interested in meeting Phyllis, the principal, and assessing the interaction between her and the superintendent. Phyllis was big in stature and very charming, so much so that I could not help but interpret her behavior as a reaction formation. She was quite deferential to the superintendent (through my work in schools I had come to expect this kind of deference to superiors, but I always found it regressive and immature), but they presented as a united front. Their diagnosis was that the current problems really stemmed from the former principal, who ran a very loose ship. Phyllis's responsibility was to tighten the screws, preventing people from getting away with doing things as they had in the past. This strictness, according to them, led to allegations of racism against Phyllis—something they were very concerned with because the allegations resulted simply from making people do their job. I asked if they thought the former principal might be missed for reasons other than letting the staff shirk its responsibility. Though they dismissed my question, I introduced the issue of race in a way different from the way in which they had considered it. The meeting ended with two commitments: I would visit the school next week, and Ted, Phyllis, and I would meet regularly to discuss the consultation. This was another attempt at keeping Ted in the picture. Though he reminded me how busy he was, Ted agreed to meet.

I was upset after this session. They had introduced the issue of race subtly, yet in a devastating fashion. The staff, predominately Black, were not doing their job according to the principal and the superintendent, and this had been allowed under the former leadership of a Black man. Now, a White woman was making them do their job, and for this she was being called a racist. It's an argument heard all too often from White supervisors: when Black supervisees are asked by White supervisors to do something they don't want to do, Blacks resort immediately to allegations of racism. I, on the other hand, did not underestimate the staff's grief over the loss of the former principal as well as his replacement by a White principal in a school in which the student body was 100% non-White and the staff 75% non-White. I assessed both Phyllis and Ted at the disintegration stage of White racial identity. They were very much aware of racial issues but found them uncomfortable and disconcerting, and they were wishing they didn't exist. Phyllis, because of the pressure she was under, could easily move into the reintegration stage, which would increase her problems of dealing with any non-White staff who were beyond the conformity stage. I found myself becoming more modest in my expectations as to what a consultation in this environment could accomplish.

Data Collection

I visited the school at the appointed time and date, only to be told by the secretary that Phyllis was not in the building and would be back short-ly. As a consultant, I had become accustomed to this kind of treatment. Leaders in trouble often resorted—perhaps not so consciously—to ways of invalidating me. I, in turn, resorted to rationalization, telling myself I could use the time to do some informal data gathering through observation.

The principal's office, where I was waiting, seemed to be tightly con-trolled and organized, with the secretary as gatekeeper of strict access to the principal. I was told simply to wait, and I almost felt chastised, as if a stu-dent. I finally said I needed to go the men's room, knowing this would give me a chance to experience some of the building. The rest of the school was quite a contrast to the principal's office: messy, dirty, and a bit out of con-trol in the hallways. I hypothesized from this that Phyllis kept a strict boundary around her office, shielding herself from the turmoil raging about her. What she didn't know or see wouldn't hurt her. This hypothesis tempered even more my enthusiasm for a successful consultation.

After my waiting an inordinate amount of time, Phyllis returned, only to tell me that she would be with me in a few minutes. I felt myself getting angry at this point and knew such feelings were diagnostically important.

Phyllis. I finally made it into the inner sanctum of Phyllis's office, only to be greeted abruptly with a question: "So, what is it you're supposed to do today?" I reminded myself quickly that I was not the one with the problem, that she was. I responded quickly: "It would be helpful if you could tell me all that you can about the problems you're having with your staff." Well, this seemed to open the floodgates, and Phyllis began talking about a select group of Blacks who were out to get her, and the union representative who was frustrating her at every turn. Phyllis came across as cynical, nasty, and angry—anything but the charmer I had experienced with the superintendent. This borderline narcissism frightened me, and I concluded that paranoid anxiety probably ran rampant in this institution. Phyllis cautioned that she had very good relationships with many of her staff, that the problems stemmed from this select group. Phyllis's affect convinced me that she may well be into the reintegration stage of racial identity. Furthermore, this select group she kept referring to could be a group of non-Whites at the resistance stage. This would constitute a crossed relationship and be responsible for the antagonism and seemingly hopeless situation.

The Staff. Phyllis's mention of the union representative convinced me that he was a key figure in the school and my interviewing of staff had best start with him; I arranged a meeting. He was White, affable, yet very direct, and his voice resonated with hostility. Larry (the union leader) told me that he had heard of my presence in the school and had instructed the union members not to talk with me. He was kind enough to give me the reason: Currently, there were many official grievances filed by staff with the union against the principal, and speaking with an outsider could undermine the process. I disagreed, explained my role and issues of confidentiality, but Larry was adamant.

Diagnosis

It was evident that the school was an organization presently paralyzed by paranoid anxiety. Phyllis's strict boundary around her office and Larry's strict boundary around the staff created an extreme "us against them" mentality. My presence meant for both Phyllis and staff an opportunity to break through the organizational defense mechanism of paranoid anxiety, but neither side appeared ready for this. It was too threatening. They had settled into a fight/flight mentality, and this was a comfortable and reassuring defense at the present moment.

I gave up all hope of conducting a process-oriented consultation. Neither the administration nor the staff were in a position to collaborate with me in conducting a diagnosis, developing strategies, or implementing solutions. I decided to move the consultation toward the purchase-of-expertise model (Schein, 1978). I agreed with the diagnosis of racial issues being at the forefront. I was also convinced that Phyllis's racial identity status only exacerbated the problem. I continued to hypothesize that the select group causing the problems was a group of non–Whites at the resistance stage. Therefore, what the staff saw as a racist principal and the principal saw as a staff of irresponsible non–Whites, I saw as issues of crossed racial identity development.

Intervention

I decided that the only possibility at this point was an intervention that would raise the consciousness of both administration and staff regarding issues of racial identity. A colleague of mine, a Black woman, and I had conducted several workshops on racial identity development. They had been quite successful, fun, and interesting.

The school always had scheduled time for staff development, so I suggested to Phyllis and the superintendent that we conduct one of these workshops. I explained that it had to do with issues of racial and cultural diversity, and they agreed, since that's how they originally framed the problem.

The workshop begins with a series of role plays between Cynthia (my colleague) and myself, as we enact different racial identity statuses and alternate roles of supervisor and supervisee. Participants then have a chance to assess their own level of racial identity development using Helms's *Race Is a Nice Thing to Have* (1992). Finally, a theoretical overview of racial identity development is given.

Results

Most of the staff and administration attended, since attendance is mandated for staff development. We quickly captured the audience's attention with the role play and by making race an immediate issue. My experience of doing staff development in schools is that one must be careful with schedule as teachers are anxious to leave at the appointed time. Therefore, the presentation was organized exceptionally well, and we began and ended on time. I had a good feeling about the workshop, knowing that my only goal was to get staff and administration to start thinking in a different way about issues of racial and cultural diversity and to begin their own process of self-awareness. Any chance of continuing the consultation would depend on whether the workshop diminished even slightly the paranoid defenses currently existing throughout the institution.

Conclusion

After the workshop, I contacted the superintendent and told him that there was little more I could do unless I heard back from Phyllis. I never heard from Phyllis, but several days after the workshop I did receive a call from Larry, the union rep, to tell me how much the staff enjoyed the workshop. I was gratified by Larry's call, in spite of his reiterating that his position remained the same regarding my talking with the staff. I again expressed my dismay, but also said it would be difficult for me to do anything more without Phyllis's initiative. Larry's call confirmed for me my feelings that the workshop could have begun a process with the staff leading to results down the road. The school year ended without any further consultation on my part. I later discovered that Phyllis was not to return as principal the following academic year.

Phyllis's leaving was probably not a bad thing. She generated in me feelings of anger, and I believe she was probably quite provocative with staff. At times, consultants must be modest in their expectations. Upon reflection, this was an example of waiting too long to get help. By the time I arrived on the scene, the situation had escalated and generated strong feelings of animosity. Nothing short of a long-term commitment by the administration, the staff, and myself to resolving the problems would have worked. This school at the present time was not capable of making such a commitment. Thus, the situation was resolved as it is in most all paranoid institutions—with one side overcoming the other. I'm sure in this case Phyllis's not returning was seen as a victory by staff. I, on the other hand, believed that the next principal had to be someone sensitive to racial issues and cultural identity, and I sincerely hoped that would be the case. There was anger among the staff, and a leader was needed who could tolerate such feelings and eventually get beyond them. Phyllis made the mistake of becoming defensive, escalating the paranoia, and drawing an overly strict boundary between herself and the staff. Her administration was doomed to fail.

SUMMARY

This chapter has charted for counselors relatively new waters of organizational consultation and development. The nature of organizations allows counselors to apply their skills to yet another level of human interaction, namely intergroup. Organizational groups are for the most part determined by members performing a common function for the organization. However, persons' culture (e.g., gender) may predetermine which organizational groups are open to them, while their role in their family of origin may affect how they behave in the work group. Organizations differ according to structure and leadership. Overbounded versus underbounded organizations have their parallels in disengaged versus enmeshed families.

Organizational consultants face a series of challenges beginning with how and through whom they enter the organization. Entering through anyone less than the real players usually dooms the consultation from the start. Having successfully entered the organization, the consultant then must perform an organizational diagnosis that concludes with a working note to the client. If the consultation is to continue, the consultant then must manage the change, along with the numerous forms of resistance generated by members of the organization. Both case examples illustrated such resistance, as well as the fact that many consultations are not carried through to completion.

As organizational membership becomes increasingly diversified, counselors armed with knowledge of intergroup relations and cultural identity development can respond to the growing need to help culturally diverse organizations become more cohesive and ultimately more productive.

REFERENCES

Adorno, T.W., Frenkel-Brunswick, E., Levinson, A.J., & Sonford, R.N. (1950). *The authoritarian personality.* New York: Harper.

Alderfer, C.P. (1976). Boundary relations and organizational diagnosis. In H. Meltzer & F.R. Wickert (Eds.), *Humanizing organizational behavior* (pp. 109–133). Springfield, IL: Charles C. Thomas.

Alderfer, C.P. (1980). The methodology of organizational diagnosis. *Professional Psychology, 11,* 459–468.

Alderfer, C.P. (1986). An intergroup perspective on group dynamics. In J. Lorsch (Ed.), *Handbook of organizational behavior* (pp. 190–220). Englewood Cliffs, NJ: Prentice-Hall.

Bain, A. (1981). Presenting problems in social consultancy: Three case histories concerning the selection of managers. *Human Relations, 34,* 643–657.

Bartee, E.M., & Cheyunski, F. (1977). A methodology for process-oriented organizational diagnosis. *The Journal of Applied Behavioral Sciences, 12,* 53–68.

Bayes, M., & Newton, P.M. (1978). Women in authority: A sociological analysis. *Journal of Applied Behavioral Science, 14,* 7–20.

Beckhard, R. (1969). *Organizational development: Strategies and models.* Boston: Addison-Wesley.

Berg, D.N. (1977). Failure at entry. In P.H. Mirvis & D.N. Berg (Eds.), *Failures in organizations: Development and change* (pp. 33–55). New York: J. Wiley & Sons.

Bion, W.R. (1959). *Experience in groups.* New York: Basic Books.

Gilmore, T.N., & Krantz, J. (1985). Projective identification in the consulting relationship: Exploring the unconscious dimensions of a client system. *Human Relations, 38,* 1159–1177.

Gould, L.J. (1989). *Exploring the origins of personal authority.* Paper presented at the Ninth Scientific Meeting of the A.K. Rice Institute, New York.

Helms, J.E. (1992). Race is a nice thing to have: A guide to being a White person or understanding White persons in your life. Topeka, KS: Content Communications.

Hirschhorn, L. (1988). *The workplace within.* Cambridge, MA: MIT Press.

Hymowitz, C., & Schellhardt, T.D. (1986, March 24). The glass ceiling. *The Wall Street Journal,* pp. 1D, 4D–5D.

Jackson, B.W., & Holvino, E. (1988). Developing multicultural organizations. *Journal of Religion and Applied Behavioral Sciences, 9,* 14–19.

Jaques, E. (1955). Social systems as a defense against persecutory and depressive anxiety. In M. Klein, P. Heimann, & R. Money-Kyrle (Eds.), *New directions in psychoanalysis.* New York: Basic Books.

Kernberg, O. (1985). *Internal world and external reality, Part III: The individual in groups.* Northvale, NJ: Jason Aronson.

Levinson, D.J. (1959). Role, personality, and social structure in the organizational setting. *Journal of Abnormal Social Psychology, 58,* 170–180.

Miller, E.J., & Rice, A.K. (1967). *Systems of organizations: Task and sentient groups.* London: Tavistock Publications.

Morrison, A.M., & Von Glinow, M.A. (1990). Women and minorities in management. *American Psychologist, 45,* 200–208.

Nadler, D.A. (1981). Managing organizational change: An integrative perspective. *Journal of Applied Behavioral Science, 17,* 191–211.

Rockwood, G.F. (1993). Edgar Schein's process versus content consultation models. *Journal of Counseling and Development, 71,* 636–638.

Roethlisberger, F. J., & Dickson, W. J. (1939). *Management and the worker.* Cambridge, MA: Harvard University Press.

Schachtel, Z. (1990, May). *Reflections on the relation between role and sense of self.* Paper presented at the Westchester Center for the Study of Psychoanalysis and Psychotherapy, Westchester, NY.

Schein, E.H. (1969). *Process consultation.* Reading, MA: Addison-Wesley.

Schein, E.H. (1978). The role of the consultant: Content expert or process facilitator. *The Personnel and Guidance Journal, 56,* 339–345.

Schneider, S.C. (1991). Managing boundaries in organizations. In K. DeVries & F.R. Manfred (Eds.), *Organizations on the couch: Clinical perspectives on organizational behavior and change.* San Francisco: Jossey-Bass.

Singer, D.L, & Shapiro, E.R. (1989, April). *Discovering the links between early family roles and current organizational roles: A loved and feared task.* Paper presented at the Spring Symposium of the Center for the Study of Groups and Social Systems, Boston.

Sue, D.W. (1995). Multicultural organizational development. In J.G. Ponterotto, J.M. Casas, L.A. Suzuki, & C.M. Alexander (Eds.), *Handbook of multicultural counseling* (pp. 474–492). Newbury Park, CA: Sage.

Weisbord, M.R. (1976). Organizational diagnosis: Six places to look for trouble with or without a theory. *Group and Organizational Studies, 1,* 430–447.

—✧✧✧—

CHAPTER 8

CONCLUSION

ETIC VERSUS EMIC DEBATE REVISITED

Recently, an article appeared in *The Counseling Psychologist* attempting to resolve the etic versus emic debate by using a common factors approach to multicultural counseling (Fischer, Jome, & Atkinson, 1998). The authors propose four factors for framing the literature on multicultural counseling: the therapeutic relationship, shared worldview, client expectations, and ritual or intervention. In other words, successful multicultural counseling can be reduced to the establishment of a good working alliance, counselor and client sharing the same worldview, the client's belief that counseling will be helpful, and the counselor's use of interventions sensitive to the client's culture. Multiculturalism, as a given form of counseling, will possess the common curative factors found in all counseling.

The purpose of mentioning this article is to convince the reader that multicultural counseling now enjoys various schools of thought and a multiplicity of viewpoints. This book has represented one focus among many and has relied upon two fundamental paradigms for providing sensitive multicultural counseling, namely second-culture acquisition and racial/cultural identity development. Furthermore, it has tried to identify some transcultural ingredients for various counseling modalities and to render them more culturally sensitive. In this sense, the book has taken a transcultural approach, because the understanding of multiculturalism is not another form of counseling among many. This seems to be the implication of the Fischer et al. (1998) article as it examines and compares multicultural counseling with other forms of counseling. This book concludes with an understanding of multiculturalism as a way of being in the world. It is a way of understanding oneself and others as the product of multiple cultural identities, some more salient than others. These identities and their salience are undergoing constant development and change resulting in the evolution of new and different cognition and emotions. The foundation of this book has been a comprehensive explanation of two constructs as a basis for counselors to understand these changes in both themselves and their clients.

Yes! All counseling is multicultural! All counseling can and should pass through the lens of multiculturalism. All counselors should be informed by the following heuristic frameworks: How is this client culturally both similar and dissimilar to myself? What are the implications of this for the counseling process? Thus, multicultural counseling is not a theory that coexists beside other theories—composing a menu of choice for the counselor. Rather, all counseling theory must be held accountable for its ability to practice a counseling sensitive to clients of diverse cultural backgrounds.

However, one aspect of multicultural counseling needs to be distinguished, that is counseling with underrepresented groups. Though all counseling can be considered multicultural, not all multicultural counseling is with underrepresented groups. There are those who wish to reserve the term *multicultural counseling* for counseling with underrepresented groups. This book has not taken that position but recognizes underrepresented groups as forming a special subpopulation for counselors. Counselors need to keep in mind two things when working with those from nondominant cultures: first, the alienation and oppression resulting from nondominant status and the unjust structures of our society that foster and maintain such oppression; second, the relationship between the client's nondominant culture and society's dominant culture. The first aspect can be examined through the framework of racial/cultural identity development; the second through the framework of second-culture acquisition. Furthermore, if counselors themselves are representative of the dominant culture, they must be super-sensitive to how their cultural status affects the counseling relationship. White racial identity development (White being a metaphor for dominant) is a helpful framework for increasing this sensitivity.

Returning for a moment to the common factors approach, there is little doubt that the development of a working alliance (i.e., the therapeutic relationship) is a key healing factor across all forms of counseling. It's hard to imagine any effective therapy taking place without a trusting relationship. In fact, it seems possible to reduce the four factors mentioned by Fischer et al. (1998) to one—that of the therapeutic relationship. I agree that counseling microskills, in so far as they contribute to developing the therapeutic relationship, have their place in multicultural counseling. However, consistent with my philosophy, they too must be submitted to a multicultural critique (as was done in Chapter 4) because *how* a therapeutic relationship is best established may vary depending on the client's cultural background.

The second common factor mentioned by Fisher et al. (1998) is shared worldview. The authors state that it is important for the counselor to share the worldview of the client in order for counseling to be effective. If this means understanding the client from the client's shoes, then it can be considered a form of empathy. However, if it means that the counselor must adopt the client worldview to be effective, this would appear to take away the dialogical and intersubjective nature of the counseling process. The position taken here is that counselor and client can have different worldviews and that this difference, instead of being alienating and promoting ineffectiveness, can actually be used to facilitate a new cultural narrative as both client and counselor learn from each other. Arredondo (1998), responding to Fischer et al. (1998), objects to their constant reference to the clinician as healer since this suggests an inequitable relationship with the client. My position is consistent with Arredondo's: Counselor and client are in a mutually enriching endeavor in which both are led to examine their cultural identities and bicultural effectiveness.

While it is true that many clients will look to counselors as experts, which may require them to adopt such a role for a limited period of time for the sake of building the therapeutic relationship, the ultimate goal is to empower the client. The relationship can be compared to that of supervisor and supervisee; the supervisee may be very dependent upon the supervisor initially, but the relationship gradually evolves into one of colleagueship and collaboration.

MULTICULTURALISM AND CONSTRUCTIVISM REVISITED

Perhaps the most arguable aspect of this book has been an initial attempt to reconcile multiculturalism with constructivism. There are those in the field who feel this is not possible, inasmuch as radical constructivism eschews culture as enslaving and falsifying the true self. This book maintains that less than radical constructivism (social constructionism, for example) is reconcilable with multiculturalism. In its most simplistic form, this reconciliation is based on the following: Because there are many cultures and cultural identities, there are many constructions of reality. Constructions of reality and worldviews can be seen as two ways of saying the same thing.

More problematic is the reconciliation of constructivism with developmental models—such as racial identity development—which are seen as positivistic. The positing of development as being the same for all would be at odds with a philosophy such as consructivism, which says that each client is unique, with a unique cultural narrative. The counselor who begins to frame such narratives within categories or stages or statuses, as racial identity development would have us do, is no longer working in a collaborative endeavor with the client to facilitate a new and more integrated cultural narrative.

A comprehensive answer to this argument is beyond the scope of this book. Let it suffice for now that I have borrowed from social constructionism in order to expose multicultural counseling as a dynamic exchange of worldviews between counselor and client. By understanding one another and listening for similarities and differences that are allowed to exist, the counseling encounter becomes a microcosm and a catalyst for the mosaical society in the making. This society where different cultures are allowed to exist side by side, enriching and beautifying one another without losing their own identities, takes place in a more intense yet perhaps less visible way in the counseling process. As the topic has progressed beyond individual to group and family counseling, this mosaical microcosm of the counseling process has been increasingly evident thus arguing that multliculturalism in counseling should be a contributing force to the process of forming a true multicultural society.

This formation cannot be accomplished with the counselor only knowing and understanding the *client's* culture. It is no accident that the multicultural counseling competencies (Arredondo, Toporek, Brown, Jones, Locke, Sanchez, & Stadler, 1996) began with awareness by counselors of their own cultural values and beliefs followed by their awareness of the client's worldview. Moreover, the structure of this book reflects the prioritized structure of the multicultural competencies. Chapters 2 and 3, "The Second-Culture Acquisition Process" and "Cultural Identity Development," were intended to help counselors understand themselves as well their clients. It is not necessary to separate neatly knowledge of self from knowledge of client. The dynamic approach to multicultural counseling taken here rests on the premise that one way counselors come to know and understand more about their own cultural identity is by carefully understanding that of their clients. The racial/cultural identity development paradigm serves to understand clients less in individualistic and intrapsychic fashion and more in terms of their attitude and relationship to their own cultural referent group. This social dimension of the cultural identity development paradigm is the key to reconciling it with social constructionism.

THE PSYCHODYNAMIC APPROACH AND MULTICULTURALISM

I have made significant use of psychodynamic principles: object relations theory, Bion's analysis of groups, organizational defenses, and transference and countertransference in the counseling process. It's unusual to find a multicultural counseling book with such heavy reliance upon psychodynamic principles. There's a tendency to view psychoanalysis and its derivatives as representing the most traditional forms of counseling, the status quo, and therefore incompatible with forms of counseling designed to better serve underrepresented groups; and there is truth to this belief. Psychodynamic approaches have focused their treatment efforts on the intrapsychic makeup of an individual, and, for the most part, they have disregarded societal forces of oppression, prejudice, and racism afflicting many nondominant groups. Multicultural counseling not only recognizes such forces but takes seriously individuals' relationship with their own cultural referent group and other cultural groups existing in their milieu. On the other hand, I have maintained that certain principles of psychodynamic theory have an etic quality and can contribute to the effectiveness of multicultural counseling.

There is little doubt that people who look and act differently than ourselves generate out-of-awareness dynamics. Psychoanalysis has used the principles of transference and countertransference to explain such dynamics. The contact stage of White racial identity development is really a paradigmatic expression of this out of awareness. Racial identity development theory, in general, is very dynamic (recall Helms's, 1995, change from the use of stages to statuses to emphasize the more dynamic nature of her theory) and has served eloquently to help both counselors and counselees understand issues of transference and countertransference in terms of race and culture. Much like Freud's theory of psychosexual development, racial identity development theory is both dynamic and epigenetic—where movement to a higher status requires successful resolution of the conflict associated with a lower status. Unlike Freud's theory, racial identity development moves the understanding of the individual out of the realms of the intrapersonal and interpersonal to those of the intragroup and intergroup, where group is defined by race and culture.

Racial identity development theory remains a work in progress, as new and emerging empirical data contribute to its refinement (see, for example, Fischer, Tokar, & Serna, 1998, for an empirical update on the RIAS). In spite of its being a work in progress and containing conflicting empirical data on some scales, one must remember that a theory so dynamically rich will cause problems for traditional forms of measurement. Furthermore, questions about a scale's validity do not necessarily invalidate the theory from which the scale is derived. No one dismissed Freud's theory of psychosexual development because of a lack of empirically valid scales with which to measure it. In an age where the defense of psychology seems to rest solely upon quantitative investigation, racial identity theory has undergone and continues to undergo statistical scrutiny. However, much like many psychoanalytic theories, racial identity development is rich, provocative, and timely. For these reasons, it has had and will have a great deal of impact upon counseling. Is it the final word? Absolutely not! Rather, it is another narration for understanding the human journey. It is timely because today that journey travels a road of ever-increasing diversity. Racial identity development theory not only serves to navigate the road better but also helps travelers to be enriched by its beauty and its splendor.

It is my sincerest hope that this book may have contributed to making that journey all the more interesting and enjoyable.

REFERENCES

Arredondo, P. (1998). Integrating multicultural counseling competencies and universal helping conditions in culture-specific contexts. *Journal of Counseling Psychology, 26,* 592–601.

Arredondo, P., Toporek, R., Brown, S.P., Jones, J., Locke, D., Sanchez, J., & Stadler, H. (1996). Operationalization of the multicultural counseling competencies. *Journal of Multicultural Counseling and Development, 24,* 42–78.

Bion, W.R. (1961). *Experience in groups.* New York: Basic Books.

Fischer, A.R., Jome, L.M., & Atkinson, D.R. (1998). Reconceptualizing multicultural counseling: Universal healing conditions in a culturally specific context. *Journal of Counseling Psychology, 26,* 525–587.

Fischer, A.R., Tokar, D.M., & Serna, G.S. (1998). Validity and construct contamination of the Racial Identity Attitude Scale—Long Form. *Journal of Counseling Psychology, 45,* 212–224.

Helms, J.E. (1995). An update of Helms's white and people of color racial identity models. In J.G. Ponterotto, J.M. Casas, L.A. Suzuki, & C.M. Alexander (Eds.), *Handbook of multicultural counseling* (pp. 181–198). Thousand Oaks, CA: Sage.

INDEX

AAAS. *See* African American Acculturation Scale (AAAS)

Accommodate, defined, 33

Accommodation, 34

Acculturation, measures of, 40–43

Acculturation model, of cultural adaptation, 27

Acculturation Rating Scale for Mexican Americans (ARSMA), 40–41

ARSMA-II and, 43

Acculturative stress

culture shock and, 37

mental health and, 36–39

models of, 37–39

Achieved racial consciousness, 56

Acosta, F.X., 108

Active preencounter stage, 51

Activity, 20

Adaptation

alternation as, 27

assimilation as, 26

cultural, 25–28

integration as, 26–27

marginality as, 28

rejection as, 27–28

Adorno, T.W., 152

Affect. *See also* Empathy

reflection skills and, 77

Affiliation variables, 19

Affirmative action organization, 163

Africa. *See* Nigrescence

African American Acculturation Scale (AAAS), 42–43

Afrocentric Movement, 51

Ahuna, C., 41

Alderfer, C.P., 148, 154, 155, 158, 165

Alonso, A., 101, 106

Alternation model, of cultural adaptation, 27

Anderson, J., 40

Anderson, L.P., 37, 38–39

Anderson, L.E., 36, 37

Anglo Orientation Subscale (AOS), 43

Anthropological concept of culture, 12

Antokoletz, J.C., 29, 30, 31

Anxiety. *See also* Group(s)

management of, 173

social systems as defenses against, 149–150

AOS. *See* Anglo Orientation Subscale (AOS)

Applegate, J.S., 29, 30

Arnold, B., 40, 41, 43

Arrendondo, P., 187, 189

ARSMA. *See* Acculturation Rating Scale for Mexican Americans (ARSMA)

Assimilation, of new experiences, 33–34

Assimilation model, of cultural adaptation, 26

Atkinson, D.R., 3, 4, 9, 43, 52, 55, 56, 58, 60, 64, 185

Attending skills, 74

Attitudes, 47

Authority, in organizations, 152–154

Autonomy stage

family counseling and, 134

of White racial identity development, 54

Avoidant type, of unachieved White racial consciousness, 56

Bain, A., 154, 156

Baker, C.E., 63

Bartee, E.M., 154

Bayes, M., 165

Beckhard, R., 158

Behavior(s), 47

attending, 74

MULTICULTURALISM IN COUNSELING
Edited by John Beasley
Production supervision by Kim Vander Steen
Designed by Jeanne Calabrese Design, River Forest, Illinois
Composition by Point West, Inc., Carol Stream, Illinois
Paper, Finch Opaque
Printed and bound by McNaughton & Gunn, Saline, Michigan